RAND

Defense Downsizing

An Evaluation of Alternative Voluntary Separation Payments to Military Personnel

David W. Grissmer,
Richard L. Eisenman,
William W. Taylor

Prepared for the
Office of the Secretary of Defense
United States Army

National Defense Research Institute
Arroyo Center

This report documents RAND's research on one aspect of the personnel drawdown, namely, how to structure voluntary separation offers to service members to efficiently meet force-reduction objectives. We develop a methodology for estimating the acceptance rate of voluntary separation offers, and we apply this methodology to evaluate a range of such offers. This document should interest those in the Office of the Secretary of Defense, military personnel policymakers, and Congressional staffs involved in implementing the personnel drawdown.

This research on separation compensation evolved from a larger project on managing the enlisted force during the drawdown. The research being reported here was carried out before development of the voluntary separation programs initiated between 1992 and 1994 and was instrumental in shaping them. The study was undertaken for the Office of the Assistant Secretary of Defense (Force Management and Personnel). It was also supported by the Deputy Chief of Staff for Personnel for the Army and was conducted jointly by the Defense Manpower Research Center, part of RAND's National Defense Research Institute (NDRI), and the Arroyo Center. NDRI is a federally funded research and development center sponsored by the Office of the Secretary of Defense, the Joint Staff, and the defense agencies. The Arroyo Center is a federally funded research and development center sponsored by the United States Army.

CONTENTS

FIGURES

BACKGROUND AND SCOPE

Changes in the military threats to the United States have radically altered the assumptions underpinning our defense policy, leading to a reexamination of the required size and mix of military forces. The size of military forces had been predicated on a NATO scenario based on the combined threat from the Soviet Union and the Warsaw Pact. However, the collapse of this threat allows the United States to maintain a smaller military force. Downsizing our military forces began in FY92 and is scheduled to continue through at least FY99.

This report presents analysis, conducted at the beginning of this drawdown, evaluating alternative strategies for achieving personnel reductions, including alternative voluntary separation offers and their utility in achieving the required reductions in personnel end-strength. Specifically, it first addresses the question of what part of the reductions should come from lowered accession levels and what part from increased separations of personnel currently in the service. It then addresses the process of how to structure separation offers to get both the number and type of desired departures as cost effectively as possible. It identifies the criteria that any separation plan should meet, evaluates proposed plans in terms of the cost to the government and perceived worth to the individual, and develops an analytic framework that the services could use as a tool to structure separation offers. The framework provides a way to estimate acceptance rates for various plans and to identify specific groups to achieve those rates.

METHODOLOGY

We first evaluate the effects of accession reductions only and also of a combination of accession reductions and increased separations of personnel with less than 20 years of service. We evaluate the future experience profiles resulting from each approach and estimate the number of additional separations required by years of service assuming a steady-state, sustaining level of accessions. We then evaluate various types of voluntary separation offers as to their utility in achieving the required reductions.

The methodology to evaluate separation offers compares the present values of each choice available to military personnel: to stay in service or to accept a voluntary separation offer. Calculating the present values of these alternatives requires key assumptions about the service member's future pay level, promotion opportunity, and probability of being allowed to stay in service until retirement. It also depends on the civilian opportunities available to the service member, his or her valuation of military health benefits, and his or her discount rate for future compensation. The report first makes assumptions about these parameters and then performs a sensitivity analysis to alternative values of these parameters. The key assumptions in the analysis are:

- the assumed value of the mean and standard deviation of military personnel discount rates at different years of service,

- the perceived mean value of military retirement benefits (health, commissary, and exchanges),

- the subjective probability that individuals from each year of service assign to their chances of actually reaching retirement eligibility,

- their assessment of their promotion opportunities if they continue,

- their perceived civilian earnings opportunities, and

- the assumed quality of military personnel within and between groups, defined by years of service and grade.

We assume in the analysis that the quality of military personnel varies only by years of service and rate of promotion. We assume that lower-quality year of service groups can be identified by looking at the pace of previous promotion—those lagging in promotion will be of lower quality than those with a history of faster promotion. We assume that all personnel within a given year of service and with a similar promotion history are of equal quality. We further assume that discount rates vary only by year of service and do not depend on previous promotion history. Some of our results are sensitive to the particular assumptions made in this analysis, and we have included a detailed sensitivity analysis to illustrate this phenomenon.

RESULTS

A Mix of Accession Reductions and Increased Separations Is Needed

Reducing personnel endstrength solely through reduced accessions would require accession levels far below those likely needed—assuming FY87–FY89 continuation rates—to support future requirements for senior personnel in the Army and Air Force. Such a policy would likely create a serious shortage of senior personnel in 10–15 years even at the lower post-drawdown endstrength levels. It would also make a force buildup at that time nearly impossible.

Thus, drawdown policies should require a mix of increased separations from personnel currently in the service and lowered accessions. Moreover, the increased separations should occur at both junior and senior levels, so that no shortages are experienced at any level in the future. Increased separations from more senior personnel will require new compensation and separation pay policies to ensure that service members are treated equitably.

New Voluntary Separation Offers Need to Be Developed

Congress placed broad restrictions on using involuntary separations as a way to achieve the drawdown. Involuntary separations could achieve the desired results, but they would not be equitable to service members under current separation pay policies. The present value of separation pay associated with involuntary separation is far below the present value of pay and benefits from continuing in service for most members with 10 or more years of service (YOS). Thus, new offers must be developed with substantially more generous separation pay if voluntary separations are to work.

Several Separation Options Are Considered

The options analyzed here include several proposed by OSD or the military services and some alternatives conceived by us. They include early vesting of retirement benefits, three variants of the Voluntary Separation Incentive (VSI) currently being implemented and two lump-sum payment options. The VSI is essentially an annuity paid over a number of years (twice the member's YOS) with annual payments equal to 2.5% x YOS x current annual pay. No health benefits or cost of living provisions are included. We also propose and analyze a few hybrid plans that include a combination of lump sums and deferred annuities.

Offers Need to Be Evaluated Using Multiple Criteria

Separation offers must be evaluated for a range of criteria that include not only the usual cost and efficiency concerns but also considerations of equitable treatment for those staying and those leaving under alternative compensation plans, namely, involuntary separation pay and normal retirement. The voluntary separation plan must be consistent with these approaches. That is, compensation for involuntary separation should not be greater than that for voluntary departure. The plan must also take account of the potential for hasty or unwise decisions by military personnel and the possibility of later regret by those who accept lump-sum payments. Finally, an important part of the cost considerations is the fact that reasonably structured separation offers will result in significant net present value savings to the government from avoidance of future retirement costs. Thus, any plan must contain provisions for recognizing these long-term savings within the DoD budget and the Congressional/Administration budget agreement.

Actual Cost and Perceived Value of Separation Offers Differ Widely

We compare the cost to the government and the perceived value to the service member of various offers. The present value of the cost to the government uses a real discount rate (the rate the government must pay for its funds) of 4 percent. There is a wide range of estimated present value costs of alternatives to the government. The current rules governing the early vesting of military personnel are the most expensive alternative in present value terms and would actually cost more than current expected retirement benefits. Adopting this alternative thus means that the government would sustain a net loss. All other approaches considered would result in net long-term savings, but their costs (not taking account of the retirement avoidance) to the government vary significantly. The VSI option, either transferable (i.e., can be sold in a commercial financial market) or nontransferable without a cost of living adjustment (COLA) is the least expensive; the lump-sum plans and VSI with COLA fall in the mid-range.

The perceived value of the plans to the individual also spans a wide range. We determine these values through a net present value computation that assumes a 12 percent real discount rate. This process means that plans having the same government present value costs but providing money sooner will look much more valuable to the individual than longer-term annuities. Thus, for equivalent government costs, the lump-sum payments or the transferable VSI plan will be preferred by the individual over nontransferable plans or annuities if the sole selection criterion is present value of future income streams.

Separation Offers Will Depend on the Size of Target Groups

Ideally, the military services need to achieve certain numbers of increased separations by years of service to maintain appropriate future experience profiles in the force. These numerical targets by YOS provide the starting point for designing separation offers. However, not all personnel within a year of service group should receive an offer. The military services must maintain a highly ready and capable force during and after the drawdown and must target voluntary separation offers so that they maintain the desired mix of occupational experience and higher-quality service members. So an important question is how to target offers within YOS groups.

Occupational targeting should include consideration of changing occupational requirements in the post-drawdown environment as well as the cost of replacing individuals in certain occupations. Other things equal, occupations with lower training costs should be targeted more heavily than those with higher training costs, and occupations with longer learning curves to achieve high levels of proficiency should be targeted less heavily than those with shorter learning curves.

The services should also make offers to personnel of lower productivity or quality. Traditionally, the services have used tenure rules to separate lower-quality service members. These tenure rules essentially separate service personnel at a given year of service into paygrade groups. Those with lower paygrade at a given YOS are judged as lower quality and are barred from continuing. Thus, the services have traditionally used speed of promotion to identify lower-quality personnel and we use that criterion in this study. We assume that personnel within a given YOS, paygrade, and occupation are of equal quality but that similar personnel in higher paygrades are of higher quality.

We find large numbers of personnel between 10 and 20 years of service in lower-grade groups. This finding is important because the size of the target groups will in part determine the acceptance rate required to obtain the necessary number of separations. Other things equal, smaller groups will require higher offers to achieve similar numbers of acceptances. The large size of lower-quality groups also avoids the important tradeoff question of whether larger offers to achieve more acceptances from lower-quality groups is preferable to lower offers that include both low- and high-quality groups.[1]

---

[1]This question—whether at the margin it is better to obtain one more acceptance by making a higher offer to a lower-quality group or to enlarge the group to include higher-quality personnel—is interesting theoretically, but the data necessary to determine this tradeoff, such as productivity differences between personnel of different quality, are not available.

Separation Offers Should Be Set to Achieve Acceptance Rates Between 20 and 60 Percent

The function of any offer is to induce to leave those who, other things being equal, would have remained in the service. We call these drawdown losses. A number of people will leave the service from a given YOS regardless of whether an offer is made. We call these normal losses. We use the cost for each separation that exceeds normal losses as the criterion to determine the optimal separation offer—a procedure that is more complex than it might seem at first.

Normal losses will accept any separation offer; money paid them will constitute a portion of the plan's cost, but their departure is not truly a benefit, because it would have happened anyway. The portion of a separation payment that goes for normal losses is part of the economic rent.[2]

A low offer that attracts few drawdown losses will still be accepted by all normal losses and will have a high percentage of economic rent. Thus, low offers mean high cost per drawdown loss. An offer can also be too high because the marginal cost per drawdown loss increases for very high offers—assuming a normal distribution of discount rates. Our method determines the "optimal" acceptance rate between these two extremes that minimizes the cost per drawdown loss.

We find that optimal acceptance rates under our assumptions using a specific Army drawdown plan fall in the 10–30 percent range for all YOS. However, we also find that curves showing the cost per drawdown remain fairly flat for offers up to around 60 percent. That is, only a small cost penalty is paid for higher-than-optimal acceptance rates. On the other hand, the cost penalty for offers below 10 percent are severe. Offers that are too low risk not achieving drawdown losses and costing significant amounts. So, given the uncertainty in the acceptance rate calculations, hedging would mean moving toward the higher acceptance rate range where the drawdown objectives are met at only small additional cost. So, we believe that it is

---

[2]Economic rent also includes amounts paid to individuals who would have left at lower offers. In this report, we consider only that portion of economic rent paid to normal losses.

better to err on the high side and that the efficient range of acceptance rates lies between 20–60 percent. Offer levels should be set by
YOS within this range. If large differences in quality exist between
target groups, then it would probably be better to have acceptance
rates of 50–60 percent for lower-quality groups than to make offers to
higher-quality groups.

We believe that within this range and under current drawdown
plans, the services can avoid targeting higher-quality groups.
Sufficient drawdown losses can probably be obtained to meet force-
shaping criteria by targeting only lower-quality or lower-skill groups.
In priority, the target for drawdown losses should be groups lagging
in promotion in the following groups;

• the 13–18 YOS group,

• the 10–12 YOS group, and

• the 7–9 YOS group.

This prioritization is based on achieving a sustainable future force
profile. The more senior groups (10–18 YOS) have the largest potential post-drawdown overages as a percentage of the total force, and
reductions here will also ensure larger savings in personnel costs and
retirement benefits. This prioritization approach also avoids more
future person-years enabling the reduction to occur with fewer
overall drawdown losses. For these reasons, the amount and type of
any separation incentive must be structured primarily for this group.
Achieving desired acceptance rates for this group should be the cornerstone of separation incentives.

Drawdown losses among more junior personnel are also needed, but
acceptance rates from the group can probably be lower, since the
year group populations are larger. It appears that acceptance rates in
the 20–35 percent range will produce the number of losses needed.
So, offers to junior personnel can be smaller because the present
value of staying is smaller and acceptance rates can be smaller as
well. However, offer amounts should be designed to keep rates
above 20 percent.

None of the DoD and Service Proposals Match All Criteria

Using the acceptance rate criteria described above, we evaluated five separation plans (Table S.1). In general, none of the plans meet the criteria of gaining higher acceptance from senior personnel and lower acceptance from junior personnel and staying within the 20–60 percent acceptance range.

Hybrid Proposals Can Be Shaped to Meet Efficiency and Equity Criteria

We propose hybrid plans containing both a lump sum and an annuity as a way to meet the above criteria. In general, hybrid plans provide the flexibility needed to shape the offers for different YOS groups. In addition, hybrid plans solve certain equity questions arising from offers. For example, an individual separated involuntarily at 7 YOS will receive a lump sum of approximately $11,000. A separation offer made to an individual at the same YOS to separate voluntarily ought to be at least as desirable and probably in the same form. For more senior individuals, say at 19 YOS, offers should not look dramatically different from retirement. A large lump sum at 19 YOS could create problems, because someone retiring at 20 YOS would receive no lump sum.

Table S.1

Evaluation of Separation Plans

Plans	Meet 20% to 60% Criterion	Rate Achieved (%)	Comments
Early retirement	No	90	Too high for all YOS
VSI transferable	No	70–80	Too high for all YOS
VSI nontransferable, without COLA	No	10–20	Too low for senior personnel
VSI nontransferable with COLA	No	50–70	Too high for junior personnel
Lump sum (2 x base)	No	10–80	Too high for junior personnel
Lump sum (2.5 x base)	No	50–95	Too high for all YOS

Hybrid plans that combine a lump sum and an annuity can meet the acceptance rate goals for the desired target groups, can address equity issues, and can offer a number of other advantages. Hybrid plans that combine lump-sum payments and deferred annuities can satisfy equity concerns at both ends of the YOS spectrum. For lower YOS, the payments might be a lump sum equal to separation pay and a deferred annuity beginning at age 65. At 19 YOS, the plan might offer a similarly computed lump sum plus an annuity starting at age 45. This approach would make the lower YOS offer similar to separation pay, but the senior YOS offer would be viewed as being similar to a retirement annuity. Our analysis has shown that the amount of the lump sum and the beginning of the annuity can be varied to achieve any desired acceptance rate. It could be shaped to provide higher acceptance rates for senior YOS and lower for junior YOS and be in the range of 20–50 percent.

Hybrid plans have several other possible advantages. They would ameliorate the long-term regret problem, since everyone would leave with a long-term annuity. The hybrid plans contain elements favored by the Office of the Secretary of Defense (OSD), the Army, and the Air Force and might provide the basis for a compromise. Finally, these plans can more easily address the problem of acceptance rate uncertainty. They could, for instance, contain an annuity portion that could not be changed but could also feature a lump-sum portion that could be empirically changed over time to achieve the desired acceptance rates.

Retirement Accrual Payments Need to Immediately Reflect Retirement Cost Savings to Offset Large Costs of Separation Payments

Early separation offers will almost surely save money for the government when the present value of avoided retirement costs is measured against the cost of separation payments. However, the savings will occur in the far term, whereas the costs occur in the short term. Thus, there may be substantial disincentives for the services to offer separation payments unless a mechanism can be found to link the long-term savings with the short-term costs. If the long-term savings are brought forward to cover the separation payment outlays and specifically given to the services making the separations, then the incentives will shift to reflect appropriate force manning decisions rather than strictly budgetary concerns.

A mechanism does exist that should link retirement savings with current outlays—the accrual retirement payments. Each year, the services pay into the retirement system an amount determined to be necessary to fund future retirements. Substantial funds have been paid in on the assumption that continuation rates would remain at pre-drawdown levels. However, the drawdown will reduce continuation rates substantially and will create a "windfall gain" for the retirement fund. Ideally, this gain would be reflected immediately in lower retirement fund payments and offset separation payments. However, the current accounting techniques used to determine fund contributions together with rules that allocate gains to the U.S. Department of the Treasury prevent this linkage. Thus, under current rules the services have to pay for separation payments by reducing funding of readiness and procurement. This is a serious deficiency in the drawdown strategy and continued effort is warranted to link retirement savings to offset separation payments.

ACRONYMS

COLA	Cost of Living Adjustment
CPI	Consumer Price Index
DoD	Department of Defense
ERISA	Employee Retirement and Income Security Act
FICA	Federal Insurance Contributions Act
HASC	House Armed Services Committee
MOS	Military Occupational Specialty
OSD	Office of the Secretary of Defense
RCP	Retention Control Point
SSB	Selective Separation Bonus
VSI	Voluntary Separation Incentive
YOS	Year(s) of Service

Chapter One

INTRODUCTION

Changes in the nature of the military threat to the United States are allowing reductions in the size of U.S. military forces. Personnel reductions of approximately 25 to 30 percent from levels existing in 1987 are scheduled. An important continuing question is how to achieve these reductions efficiently while maintaining morale and a desirable experience mix of personnel in future years.

Reducing the size of the Armed Forces is never easy and comes at a particularly difficult time in light of the successful operations in Desert Storm. Policies governing the military drawdown must take account of the services rendered to the country by military personnel, particularly senior personnel, the volunteer nature of the current Armed Forces and current fiscal constraints.

The all volunteer force and the associated set of personnel and compensation policies implemented to make it succeed makes this drawdown different and more difficult than previous major military drawdowns. Past drawdowns have usually occurred at the end of a major conflict where the draft was used to increase the size of military forces. A major part of the drawdown was accomplished by simply releasing those drafted who generally wished to return home. However, the all volunteer force consists of individuals who have voluntarily chosen military service, many of whom have planned for long military careers. None of the Armed Forces has experience in major reductions in forces in an all volunteer environment.

Over the last 20 years, policy emphasis has been to maintain a relatively stable force size by recruiting high-quality enlistees and maintaining high levels of retention. These policies have been successful in building a high-quality, very experienced force with historically high proportions of the force who plan to stay until retirement. Although these career expectations contribute to high morale and performance, they also make force reductions difficult to do in an equitable and fiscally prudent manner.

Besides the difficulty posed by an all volunteer force, developing a strategy for reducing the number of military personnel is complicated by two additional features of the military personnel system: no lateral entry and a retirement system characterized by "cliff vesting" and large retirement annuities for life. No lateral entry into the system means that requirements for all senior experienced personnel must be met by managing the flow of personnel through a long personnel pipeline starting with accessions and extending to retention over 10 or more years. In a steady-state environment where force sizes are relatively constant and retention rates and compensation policies are fairly static, this process works by simply establishing accession requirements that insure adequate numbers of senior personnel 10 to 20 years later.

When force size is reduced quickly and fewer senior personnel are needed, the pipeline built to support a much larger force will contain too many personnel. Unless reductions in force are allowed at all points in this pipeline, the only other option of achieving end-strength reductions is by reducing accessions. However, in the absence of reductions in pipeline personnel, reduction in accessions is required below levels required to sustain the necessary equilibrium flow of personnel required by the new force size. This policy would risk shortages of senior personnel in future years.

The policy of no lateral entry into the military system ideally requires drawdown policies that would reduce military personnel at all experience levels proportionately. However, the characteristics of the retirement system make it difficult to achieve reductions of personnel with more than 10 years of service. Service members completing 10–12 years of service have traditionally been protected from involuntary separations by an implicit contract. This implicit contract between the member and the service has developed because of the sudden vesting of military retirement benefits at 20 years of service together with the immediate claim on a substantial annuity and retirement benefits. Involuntary separation close to retirement eligibility would leave a member with no annuity or benefits.

In times of force size stability or growth, this implicit contract protects the services against sudden, large departures of senior personnel. However, in time of force size reductions, this implicit contract constrains personnel policymakers in making choices about how to reduce force size. Breaking this implicit contract during a drawdown period would be inequitable to service members and would lower future retention rates because members would no longer feel fully protected against involuntary separations close to retirement. Although current compensation policy calls for a separation payment equal to 10 percent of base pay for each year of service, this amount is far below the expected retirement benefits for members within 10 years of retirement.

Although involuntary separation of these personnel would violate the implicit contract, a voluntary separation before retirement eligibility would be acceptable if members perceive separation incentives as more desirable than expected retirement benefits. This report evaluates a range of specific compensation alternatives for making voluntary reductions in service personnel during the drawdown.

RELATED RESEARCH

This report continues RAND research directed at personnel and budgetary policy issues arising from the military drawdown. The initial work evaluated various issues and strategies for accomplishing the personnel drawdown (Grissmer and Rostker, 1992). The options evaluated included reductions accomplished only through cuts in accessions and various combinations of accession cuts and additional voluntary or involuntary separations taken at different years of service. This work was partly responsible for OSD policy guidance that limited reductions in accession levels during the drawdown. These limits made it necessary for the Army and Air Force to develop policies directed at separating large numbers of personnel currently in the service who would prefer to stay in the military. This initial research also concluded that unless these services separated personnel at all experience levels, there were risks that the future force structure would develop undesirable swings between forces having higher and lower levels of seniority.

A second area of RAND's research will address the changes needed in military retirement accrual funding during a military drawdown to reflect the reduced retirement liabilities associated with separations and lower endstrength. We recommended lower retirement contributions during the drawdown. This approach would allow reduced retirement contributions to offset separation payments in DoD budget authority. Thus, voluntary separations and the associated payments might be viewed as more feasible if there were no short-term budgetary increases.

This report addresses a third key topic in personnel drawdown policies: how to structure separation pay to induce additional voluntary losses among middle and senior personnel. This work evaluates specific types of offers. It addresses the questions of the short- and long-term costs of various offers, develops a methodology for estimating acceptance rates, and estimates acceptance rates for each offer.

ORGANIZATION

The report is divided into seven topic chapters. The topics are:

- Need for voluntary separations,
- Separation incentive options,
- Selection criteria,
- Cost and perceived value comparisons,
- Voluntary acceptance rates,
- Managing voluntary separation costs, and
- Conclusions.

We argue in Chapter Two that voluntary reductions are desirable for the services—particularly the Army and Air Force. In Chapter Three, we discuss the separation incentive options that have been proposed as well as alternatives developed by RAND. Chapter Four describes both the political and economic criteria important in evaluating a specific incentive. This analysis focuses on the government costs and the perceived value of each incentive to the member. Chapter Five presents and contrasts these costs and perceived values for each plan. The success of such plans will depend on their ability to induce the desired number of separations. Thus, a methodology is needed to estimate acceptance rates for various plans. We present this methodology in Chapter Six and identify the groups that the services would likely target for such offers. We then apply the methodology to estimate acceptance rates for the various plans. Given the acceptance rates, Chapter Seven estimates the outlays and expected future costs for certain plans. Chapter Eight provides a summary and conclusions.

Chapter Two

NEED FOR VOLUNTARY SEPARATIONS

Current drawdown plans call for reductions in military personnel strength from the FY90 level of approximately 2.0 million to 1.45 million or lower by FY99. These reductions have no precedent in the all volunteer force. Previous large reductions occurred at the end of wars when the draft had been used to build personnel endstrength. Forces were reduced mainly by lowering the level of the draft and allowing those drafted to return home. In a volunteer force, individuals choose to enlist, and historically large numbers of these enlistees have been choosing to reenlist and stay in the military to retirement after 20 years of service. This high retention together with the absence of large numbers of draftees have made today's force the most senior of any in the last 50 years.

Force reductions will require new compensation policies to address the expectations of volunteers who have entered the service planning on a full military career and military retirement. The current force has large numbers of senior individuals with 10–19 years of service, and critical policy questions include whether force reductions should include these individuals, and, if so, what separation compensation is required.

Earlier research (Grissmer and Rostker, 1992) concluded that it would be desirable to achieve the drawdown with a mix of accession reductions and reductions at all levels of personnel experience—particularly for more senior personnel. Figure 2.1 summarizes the advantages and disadvantages of reductions among experienced personnel to accomplish the drawdown.

RANDMR171-2.1

- Advantages of separations among senior service members:
  - Avoid temporary, and perhaps longer-lasting, changes in force experience mix.
  - Increase cost savings.
  - Reduce the total number of separations required.
  - Improve promotion opportunity for those remaining.

- Disadvantages of separations among senior service members:
  - No equitable separation pay has been available.
  - Separation pay may be costly in the short term.
  - Voluntary separations may risk exodus of quality personnel.
  - Involuntary separations affect morale and retention.

Figure 2.1—Advantages and Disadvantages of Senior Separations

The first advantage is that a more stable experience distribution of personnel can be maintained over time. Endstrength reductions that cut accessions for younger year of service (YOS) groups disproportionately will cause large increases in seniority in the near term and make cyclic changes in the experience distribution more likely in the future. Such cyclic changes occurred at the conclusion of the Korean War with a resulting 20-year distortion in the desired experience distribution.

Cyclic changes in the experience distribution can change force capability in undesirable ways, creating problems in the ideal matching of individuals to jobs and the maintenance of desired promotion patterns. A senior force will be capable but expensive. Senior individuals may have to perform jobs below their ability and promotion for more junior personnel may lag. A too-junior force may lower capability as rapid promotion pushes junior personnel into higher skill jobs faster than desirable.

Separation of more senior personnel also reduces costs because of lower military pay, allowances, and future retirement costs to the government. Further, these separations mean that fewer people will have to leave the service to achieve a given endstrength objective. This effect occurs because an average senior person (with 10–19 YOS) will serve more expected future manyears than more a junior person (3–8 YOS). So, not only will this year's endstrength be reduced, but future endstrengths will also be reduced. Finally, separating personnel from grades upon which numerical constraints have been imposed (essentially E-5s and E-6s) will speed up promotion for those remaining. An unbalanced drawdown that does not include these more experienced personnel sharply reduces promotion opportunity for those in the 7–12 YOS groups. Since higher-quality personnel are more sensitive to promotion opportunity, any approach that lowers promotion opportunity risks losing these people.

The major problem with separating more senior personnel is that compensation policies that allow equitable treatment and will induce voluntary separations did not exist at the beginning of the drawdown. Law in force at the beginning of the drawdown authorizes separation payments only when individuals are *involuntarily* separated with more than six years of service. Involuntary separation pay equals 10 percent of annual pay for each year of service. Even for individuals with 7–10 years of service, this formula falls far short of compensating them for the loss of pension benefits. The more senior the individual, the larger the gap. Thus, current separation payments do not come close to honoring the implicit military personnel contract.

Another barrier to senior separations is that separation payments— whether voluntary or involuntary—could increase near-term DoD outlays. If such payments were immediate and high enough to provide equitable compensation, then a large increase in near-term outlays would result, even though there may be net long-term savings. Moreover, equitable voluntary separation payments could create problems such as a large exodus of quality personnel if the target group for such a program were not carefully defined. Finally, an involuntary separation program without equitable compensation would include a large number of personnel who served with distinction in Operation Desert Storm and would surely have a detrimental effect upon the morale and retention of those remaining on active duty, which could clearly deter future recruiting for the all volunteer force.

In a drawdown, proportional reductions in accessions and in personnel inventories across all YOS are needed if a similar experience mix is desired in the future. The lower endstrength force may actually require a different experience distribution—perhaps because of changes in missions or combat/support ratios or to maintain a base of experience to rebuild a larger force. The current experience mix for each service, before the drawdown, is the most senior of any in the last 50 years and a nonproportional drawdown would bring even higher levels of seniority. Thus, it seems desirable at minimum to maintain the current experience distribution for future forces.

However, some prefer a strategy of cutting accessions disproportionately to avoid separating current personnel. This approach would increase near-term seniority even more. Although a lower inventory of personnel will require lower accession levels for sustaining long-term force experience profiles (the sustaining accession level), accession levels below the sustaining level risk having too few senior personnel in future years (see Figure 2.2).

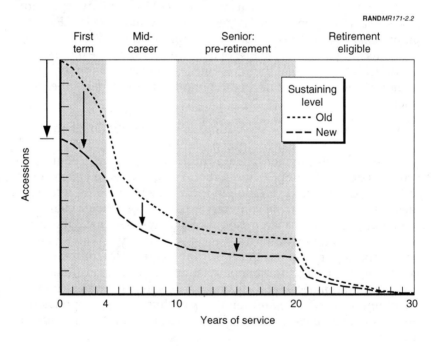

Figure 2.2—Proportional Drawdown from Illustrative Distribution

Figure 2.3 illustrates the resulting personnel experience distribution when an endstrength reduction is accomplished through cutting accessions only. Accessions are reduced to levels below those required to sustain future seniority. In the short term, this produces a smaller force with too many senior personnel. In the longer run, keeping accessions below sustaining levels risks producing too few senior personnel.

The propagation of shortages and overages over time may not be inevitable. Depending on how much the level of accessions falls below the sustaining level, it may be possible to augment the cohorts with prior service personnel or to raise retention rates through pay raises or bonus payments. However, the ability of such changes to offset the effects of a lack of accessions has limits. Moreover, lower-than-expected retention rates could shrink these cohorts even more. In general, fewer risks are incurred by accessing close to current estimates of long-term sustaining levels.

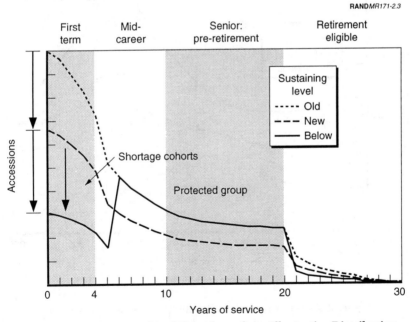

Figure 2.3—Nonproportional Drawdown from Illustrative Distribution

Figure 2.4 shows how much seniority will rise in the short term under a policy of cutting accessions only. These estimates assume an earlier House Armed Services Committee (HASC) version of the drawdown, which reduced the Army by 35 percent and the Air Force by 28 percent from FY90 to FY95. Part of the increased seniority would have occurred in the absence of the drawdown because of the higher retention of all volunteer force personnel, particularly after the large pay increases in 1980 and 1981. However, a policy of cutting accessions only significantly increases seniority for the Air Force and Army, and to a lesser extent the Navy.

Career separations will be required to maintain a stable experience mix during the drawdown. Figure 2.5 shows the results of a series of simulations using the HASC drawdown scenario for the Air Force, assuming that current continuation rates extend during the drawdown. The three scenarios assume that reductions are allowed over specific

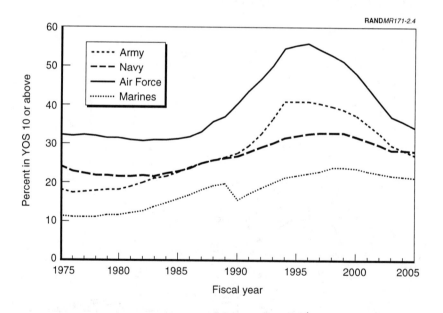

**Figure 2.4—Seniority Trends Would Increase Sharply Under
Accession-Only Drawdown**

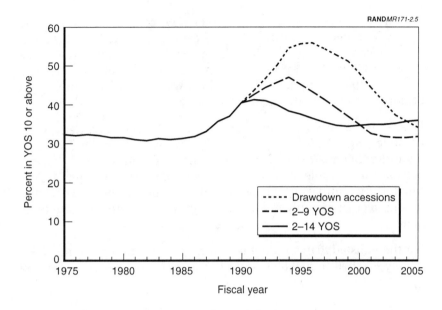

Figure 2.5—Senior Separations Are Required to Stabilize Air Force
Seniority

years of service. The accessions-only option allows only normal attrition, i.e., no increased separations. The force-shaping policies labeled 2–9 YOS and 2–14 YOS allow reductions among the designated
YOS groups. The distribution of losses within each YOS group is determined by establishing a template that reflects a "steady-state"
experience profile. This template is the steady-state, long-term
equilibrium force given that recent continuation rates continue. It is
the sustainable experience mix given current compensation policies.
Maintaining this experience mix means that the personnel force will
maintain a relatively constant junior/senior personnel experience ratio, and current compensation policies will not tend to change this
ratio over time. Each simulation takes the reductions proportionately to the current amount each YOS group exceeds the steady-state
template.

The results show that moderate stability in seniority is achieved
when reductions in the 2–14 YOS range are allowed. In fact, about

one-third of the separations in the 2–14 YOS scenario would be in the 9–14 YOS range. Seniority increases even under the 2–14 YOS scenario because we have excluded the 15–19 YOS groups from cuts. With early retirement programs, separations could also be induced in the 15–19 YOS group. This would allow an essentially unchanged seniority percentage during the drawdown.

Deeper force cuts than those assumed in the previous figures are possible. Figure 2.6 shows the Army's "excess" seniority in FY95 under different endstrength scenarios. The assumption still is that accessions are the sole means of force reduction. The overages are estimated by comparing the projected FY95 experience mix profile (under accessions-only reduction policies) to the steady-state template.

For the enlisted Army, reductions from the current level of approximately 600,000 to 450,000 could bring seniority overages of 40–60

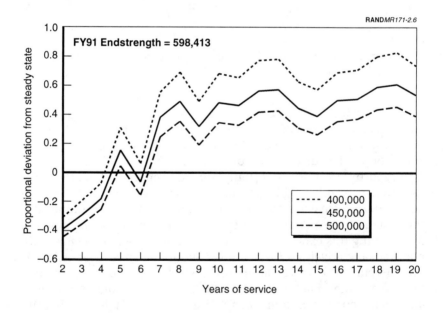

Figure 2.6—Relying on Normal Attrition Would Create Senior Overages for Both Small and Large Reductions—Army Example

percent in FY95. Current plans call for Army reductions to 450,359.
Even if the endstrength returned to 500,000, there could be 30–40
percent excess senior inventories in 1995.

The Army has generally planned reductions among mid- to senior-
level personnel to help mitigate these trends. However, Congress has
expressed concern over using involuntary separations to achieve the
drawdown losses and has restricted the services from using them for
more experienced personnel (McCain, 1991; SASC, 1991). This re-
striction means that reductions in these mid- and senior-level YOS
will not occur without an equitable voluntary separation program.

The Air Force also risks excess seniority under either small or large
reductions (Figure 2.7). Endstrength reductions to 350,000 bring excess senior inventories of 40–60 percent in FY95. Current plans call
for the Air Force to reduce to 335,000. Even if the endstrength were
as much as 400,000, excess senior inventories of 20–40 percent could

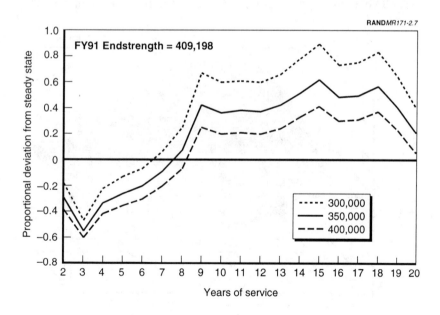

Figure 2.7—Relying on Accession-Only Cuts Would Create Senior Overages
for Both Small and Large Reductions—Enlisted Air Force Example

occur in 1995. The Air Force more so than the Army has planned to rely on reducing accessions as the primary means of achieving force reductions. This tendency is in large part due to the absence of an equitable incentive to achieve voluntary reductions.

One effect of cyclic changes in force seniority is that over time the same jobs are filled with personnel with different levels of experience. Figure 2.8 illustrates a worst-case scenario for the Air Force with accessions only cuts during drawdown and a subsequent requirement for a force buildup in FY97 to FY05.

This figure uses FY90 (the zero base line in the center of the figure) as a base case for the experience level of Air Force jobs and plots the deviation in years (plus and minus values on the vertical axis) from FY90 average experience levels by YOS for selected points in the future: 2000 and 2010. It shows, for example, that jobs held by personnel with 10 years of service in FY90 will be manned by personnel with 13 years average experience in FY95 (the bar is +3 over the 1990

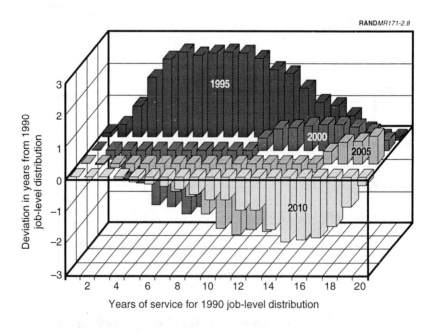

Figure 2.8—Drawdown Policies Could Shift the Experience Level
in Existing Jobs

baseline). If FY90 readiness and productivity were acceptable, then the increased cost of senior personnel may not be justified. Shifts in experience are probably riskier among more junior personnel who are still learning job skills. In FY95, jobs assigned to junior personnel would be filled by more individuals with 1 to 3 more years of experience, boosting productivity and readiness.

However, a risk is that a force buildup may be required just when the small cohorts hit the more senior ranks. In this case, the small cohorts would provide too few senior personnel for the 2005 force, and a buildup would exacerbate this problem. In this scenario, the job filled by an individual at 10 YOS in FY90 and 13 YOS in FY95 would be filled by an individual at 8 YOS in 2005. This figure illustrates that the drawdown strategy should also be formed in the light of possible buildups or further reductions after FY95.

Chapter Three

SEPARATION INCENTIVE OPTIONS

The first part of this report argued for reducing the seniority of to-day's force through separating senior personnel before they reach retirement age. The remaining part of the report will examine various compensation incentives to induce these individuals to leave the service voluntarily before reaching retirement. Congress proposed legislation that would ban involuntary separations of senior personnel during the drawdown (McCain, 1991; SASC, 1991). This ban and simple fairness make it mandatory to develop voluntary separation plans (see Figure 3.1).

RAND*MR171-3.1*

- Voluntary

- Perceived as one-time

- Service option to set eligibility by skill and grade

- Costs offset by lowered accrual contribution

- Simple and understandable

- Criteria for incentive amount offered
    - Government cost lower than expected value of current retirement
    - Perceived value high enough to attract only the desired level of separations
    - Especially attractive to those not expecting promotion
    - Avoid short-term regret for those not offered the option
    - Avoid long-term regret for those accepting the offer

Figure 3.1—Desirable Characteristics of Career Separation Policies

Since we desire only temporary changes, any policy should be perceived as limited to the drawdown period. To control the quality and skill mix of personnel leaving, the services need the authority to specify the occupation and grade levels of those eligible for voluntary offers. This authority will enable the services to prevent the exodus of large numbers of highly qualified personnel or those who have high replacement costs. Another desirable characteristic for any voluntary separation policy is that it be simple and understandable to all concerned.

Several factors combine to establish criteria for the amount that should be offered to induce voluntary senior separations. Ideally, the present value of the offers should be less than the present value of the expected retirement annuities and benefits. Below, we will show that almost all reasonable offers will yield a net present value savings to the government. The amount of the offer need only be high enough to produce the desired number of separations. Higher offers will be inefficient. Other things equal, offers should be more attractive to those in lower grades at a given YOS and those not expecting further promotions. This approach will ensure that losses will occur primarily among lower-quality groups. However, offers to individuals who would normally be separated through "up or out" or tenure policies would be inefficient. So offers should be restricted as far as possible to groups who would normally not be separated by these policies.

Finally, the offer should not be so attractive that it will create morale problems among personnel with high grade and skill levels when they are not given the offer. It must also have a low potential for long-term regret among those who accept it in lieu of military retirement. Long-term regret can occur because of misinformation or misunderstandings about the offer. It can also occur if lump-sum payments are offered and quickly spent.

Several types of separation incentive offers have been considered (Beland, March 1991; Beland, April 1991; "Military Voluntary Separation Incentive Act," 1991) (see Figure 3.2). An OSD proposal, the Voluntary Separation Incentive (VSI) plan, consists of an annuity that starts immediately upon separation and continues for a period equal to twice the service member's length of service. The initial payment is determined by the current retirement formula (.025 x

RAND*MR171-3.2*

- • Voluntary separation incentive (VSI)
  - – Annuity paid for 2 × years served
  - – Initial payment determined by current rule (.025 × YOS × final pay)
  - – No in-kind benefits
  - – Negotiable or nonnegotiable options
  - – COLA and no-COLA options
- • Early retirement
  - – Lifetime annuity
  - – Initial payment determined by current rule
  - – Full benefits and COLA
- • Lump-sum payment
- • Hybrid plans (combining lump sum and annuity)

Figure 3.2—Characteristics of Different Plans

YOS x final pay). No medical, commissary, or exchange benefits are included in this plan, although some arrangement for a transition period may be allowed. VSI does not contain cost of living adjustments (COLA). VSI was originally conceived as a negotiable instrument similar to a Treasury Bond, which the separatee could sell at the going market rate after leaving service. This meant that the future stream of payments would be discounted at rates comparable to those used for 30-year Treasury Bills, which were about 8 to 9 percent in 1992. The legislated version, however, is nonnegotiable, which means that it will be perceived by the average service member at a nominal discount rate of approximately 16 percent resulting in a much lower perceived value than that of the negotiable option.

The Army proposed an early retirement plan for more senior personnel (15–19 years of service) as an alternative. This plan consists of a lifetime annuity, starting immediately upon separation, with the initial payment also determined by the applicable rule for military retirement for the group in question, and including full benefits and full COLAs (again, as with current military retirement). The Air Force, on the other hand, preferred a lum-sum payment method, which could be related to the current separation pay authorized for involuntary separations. Involuntary separation pay provides a lump sum equal to 10 percent of final pay for each year served. The Air Force advocated increasing this amount by a factor of two or two and one-half to induce voluntary separations.

These proposals reflect deep concerns held by each service. The Army feels that acceptance rates will be low and favors a more lucrative plan to raise acceptance rates. It also favors a plan that resembles current retirement and remains opposed to lump-sum settlements, partly to prevent frivolous use and long-term regret. The Air Force is concerned that any relationship between the voluntary separation concept and current military retirement would give Congress the opportunity to review the latter, a process which could lead to further reductions in military benefits similar to those that occurred in the 1980s. The Air Force also believes that lump-sum payments would be the least expensive method for the government to achieve the desired voluntary separations and would avoid major increases in the health benefits for nonactive duty personnel. The advantages of each proposal led us also to consider plans that combine a lump-sum payment with an annuity. We will refer to these as hybrid plans.

Chapter Four

SELECTION CRITERIA

Whatever plan is chosen to reduce the size of the armed forces, it will have to meet a number of criteria. The political (Figure 4.1) and economic (Figure 4.2) categories are the two most important, and this chapter explores those in some detail.

Congress does not wish to reduce the force through new involuntary separation programs (McCain, 1991; SASC, 1991). This position does not restrict existing management policies whereby the services separate those who fail promotion, but it could prohibit tightening these policies further to achieve the drawdown.

Congress is concerned that policies to induce voluntary separations must be sufficiently equitable so as to minimize the potential for

RAND*MR171-4.1*

- No new involuntary separation programs (Congressional mandate)

- Minimize long-term regret of individuals

- Consistent with current military compensation
    - Retirement system
    - Separation pay

- Consistent with treatment of private sector workers

Figure 4.1—Political Criteria

RAND*MR171-4.2*

- Make offers sufficient to attract only desired voluntary separations

- Meet Treasury and Congressional financing and tax requirements
    - Separation payments
        - Paid for out of current outlays
        - Taxed in year of receipt
        - No FICA withheld
    - VSI payments
        - Meet scoring rules of budget committee

- DoD retirement accrual payments should reflect lowered retirement liability
    - Reduction may offset payments for DoD budget authority
    - Any payments still increase government outlays

Figure 4.2—Economic Criteria

long-term regret among those who accept the offer. Congress also legislated retirement and separation pay plans (SASC, 1991). This consistency may be desirable for reasons of equity and morale. For instance, lower-quality individuals might be offered lump sums at 19 YOS, whereas higher-quality personnel may not be given offers and thus have only the retirement option. Because of the range of discount rates among higher-quality personnel, some would have preferred the lump-sum option. This means that lower-quality personnel would be given retirement options significantly different from those given to, and perhaps preferred by, higher-quality personnel. Not only might this cause morale problems, but it is inherently inequitable to the higher-quality personnel. Thus, we believe that offers made to those at higher YOS should be structured similar to ordinary retirement rather than lump sums.

At lower YOS, the issue is somewhat different. The alternative is involuntary separation pay—a lump sum. If separation pay takes the form of annuities, some may prefer involuntary separation pay because of differing discount rates. This might create perverse incentives to lower performance to qualify for involuntary separation pay.

Developing plans that appeal to individuals at both ends of the YOS distribution may require making the plans at the lower end look more like involuntary separation pay and those at the upper end more like retirement.

Finally, Congress appears somewhat sensitive to the way that private sector workers are treated under the Employee Retirement and Income Security Act (ERISA) (SASC , 1991). This legislation mandates some vesting after only 5 years of experience with a civilian firm. Military compensation has been primarily dictated by the needs of national security rather than consistency with private sector firms, but future competitiveness with the private sector may argue for similar treatment in downsizing.

Voluntary separation offers should only be high enough to induce the required number of senior personnel in the targeted groups to leave the service. Critical tradeoffs exist among the value of the offer, the size and composition of the target group, and the quality of personnel who will leave voluntarily. Narrow target groups may be desirable to restrict offers to only low-quality personnel or occupations with low replacement costs. In general, once the characteristics and size of a target group are determined, it will require a higher separation offer to achieve a higher acceptance rate within that group. In general, the required offer for a given acceptance rate will be a function of the distribution of discount rates within the group, the distribution of outside wage and benefits in civilian life, and the perceived future wages and retirement benefits within the military. A key policy question is whether offers should be set higher allowing narrower target groups or set lower mandating expanded target groups. Thus, as a starting point for shaping offers, the services must determine where reductions are desirable and identify the relevant target groups.

Any offer must conform to Treasury, Congressional, and DoD Board of Actuaries rules and requirements. These rules can critically affect both the value of the offer to the individual and the budgetary consequences to DoD. Three questions here need examination. The first is how such separation incentives should be financed. The second is how such payments would be taxed. The third is how such payments are to be handled under the budget agreement.

For involuntary separation pay, the rules are to take the payments from current outlays, tax them in the year of receipt without withholding Federal Insurance Contributions Act (FICA), and count them as ordinary outlays under the budget agreement. However, voluntary separation pay, made to senior personnel for whom payments have been made into the Military Retirement Fund, presents some important questions concerning financing and budget agreements. These questions arise from the fact that the government will likely generate net savings from separation offers. Since there is no precedent for making these decisions, the Congressional budget committees and the DoD Board of Actuaries must decide how these questions will be handled. These decisions are fairly complex but can play an important role in evaluating the various proposals.

For instance, one proposal would pay part or all of the separation payments out of the Military Retirement Fund, offering the justification that this fund will net the savings from lower retirement liabilities. This fund exists in the Treasury account, and such a proposal would not result in new DoD outlays but would cause temporarily increased domestic outlays. Other proposals call for reducing the DoD contribution to the Military Retirement Fund over the drawdown period to reflect the reduced liability and having these reductions at least offset the separation payments from the DoD budget. However, since these reductions occur in the form of intergovernmental transfers from Defense to Treasury, any such payments will still increase overall government outlays. Thus, decisions about how such payments are scored under the budget agreements still need to be made. A further example of how these rules can critically affect both the value of the offer to the individual and the budget consequences to DoD will be seen below.

Chapter Five

COST AND PERCEIVED VALUE COMPARISONS

Before presenting our methodology for estimating acceptance rates for each proposal, we estimate the present value of the government costs and the perceived value to the individual of the plans. The plans differ markedly in the timing and the amount of payments, and the present values make it possible to compare the various offers. Present values are also an important first step in estimating the acceptance rates.

All comparisons have a standard format. The government cost per individual always appears on the left side of each figure and is based on an average real government discount rate of 4 percent. The service member's perceived value always appears on the right side of each figure and is based on an average real individual discount rate of 12 percent. The curves represent a service member's perceived value of the given separation plan. Programs considered here vary with years of service as shown in the figures.

Evaluating alternative plans requires estimating both the cost to the government and the perceived value to the individual. The former determines the effect on government expenditures, and the latter is critical in determining what level of offer will be accepted by individuals. These figures show the present value of current separation pay and expected retirement annuities. (See the appendix for a more detailed description of assumptions and formulas used in the present value calculations.) We also show the present value of expected retirement annuities including a valuation of retirement benefits (medical, commissary, and exchange). Although individuals place a unique value on a specified set of benefits, we have assumed an av-

erage value of $3000 annually. This value is close to the average an-
nual cost per retiree incurred by the government to provide these
benefits.

The calculations are for an average Army enlisted person who will retire as an E-6 at 20 YOS and who views his or her chances of reaching
retirement at a given YOS as average.[1] We assume that the individual
has the average pay level at a given YOS in estimating present values
but that the individual's final pay at 20 YOS is that of an E-6. The latter assumption is made because voluntary separation offers will
likely be made to lower-ranking individuals at a given YOS. At 20
YOS, almost all enlisted personnel are E-6 or E-7. Thus, we expect
that those taking offers would likely be E-6 at 20 YOS. We also take
account of the three different retirement annuity rules for individuals
at different YOS. The three curves on the left of Figure 5.1 show that
government costs differ substantially for separation pay and retirement and that benefits can significantly affect the costs of any offer.
The curves on the right show that the perceived present value of retirement is markedly lower at an individual's 12 percent discount
rate. Whereas the government costs are estimated at $150,000 for an
individual at 17 YOS who will retire without benefits, the member's
perception is only $55,000. This means that individuals having 12
percent discount rates would be willing to accept $55,000 now in ex-
change for their expected retirement annuity.

For offers that include annuities, the cost to the government and the
perceived value will differ substantially because the discount rate of
military personnel is much higher than the government discount
rate. This difference in discount rates is the primary reason that separation offers will result in net savings to the government.

The figures show that separation pay falls far short of the expected
value of retirement for individuals close to retirement. Separation
pay is not an equitable substitute for these individuals. However, for

---

[1]If those accepting offers do not have average probabilities of making it to retirement,
the cost and perceived value comparisons will change. However, the comparisons will
not change much for personnel over 13 years of service, since almost all personnel
plan on retirement from that point on and the variance in perceived retirement
probability is small. For younger groups, the perceived probability of making it to
retirement will have wider variance and more uncertainty occurs in comparisons.

RANDMR171-5.1

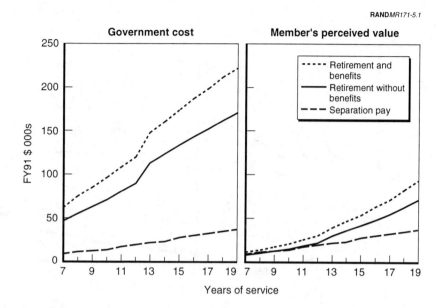

Figure 5.1—Existing Retirement Plan and Involuntary Separation Pay

individuals with less than 10 YOS, separation pay comes close to the expected value of retirement.

Next we compare the present values of the baseline voluntary separation plans discussed in the previous chapter. Early retirement at the YOS specified in Figure 5.2 (payment according to the applicable rule for the individual in question) is more costly than making no offer and allowing individuals to proceed to retirement. These increased costs result from the earlier and increased number of payments that would occur under this plan. Although the annual annuity would be less than that earned at 20 YOS, the additional payments made before the member would have reached 20 YOS more than make up for the lower annual annuity. Our analysis also suggests that members would perceive early retirement as substantially more valuable than their expected retirement benefits. Thus, an early retirement offer would be very costly and could generate higher acceptance rates than needed. Moreover, the figures show that individuals with fewer years of service would find early retirement with benefits more attractive than would those with more years of service.

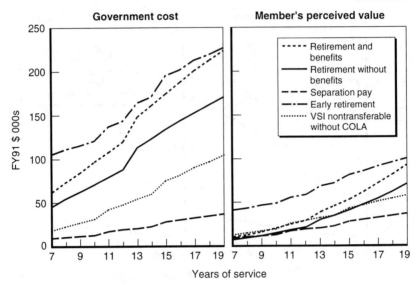

Figure 5.2—Voluntary Separation Proposals

The VSI (nontransferable without COLA) costs significantly less than the expected retirement benefits but more than a separation payment. However, the member would view the VSI option as being closer to the value of retirement than a mandatory separation pay at lower YOS, but well below the value of retirement at higher YOS. This VSI plan would primarily appeal to more junior personnel.

Our next comparison looks at three variations of the original VSI proposal (Figure 5.3). The original proposal was to view the annuity as a bond and to allow the individual to cash it in the marketplace. The cash value was determined by applying the interest rate for long-term bonds of 8 percent. Note that the cost to government is the same for the transferable and nontransferable versions (and thus the left side of the chart has only five curves), but COLA protections cause a significant cost difference. Inflation is assumed to be 4 percent for COLA calculations. From the member's viewpoint, VSI with transferability is valued more highly than the expected retirement annuity, but removing this feature substantially reduces the value to

RAND*MR171-5.3*

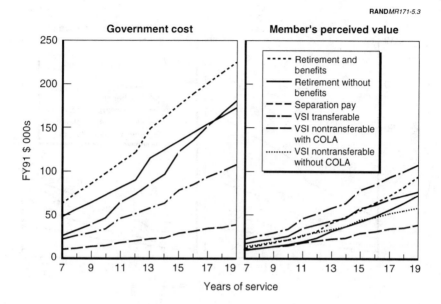

Figure 5.3—Comparison of VSI Options

the member. This is because the average member discounts the annuity at a real rate of 12 percent, but when cashable the value is discounted at the current real market rate of 8 percent. Adding the COLA feature to the nontransferable VSI boosts the value to the member closer to the expected value of retirement.

The next comparison examines lump-sum payments (Figure 5.4). Since the payments are immediate, cost and perceived value are identical. This lump-sum approach takes maximum advantage of the difference in discount rates between the government and the individual. Lump sums would be relatively low cost to the government, but their perceived value by service members is quite high. Separation offers of between 2 to 2.5 times regular separation pay provide value equivalent to expected retirement pay for YOS 7–19.

We pointed out above that the early retirement option costs more than current retirement. There are, however, alternative early vesting plans that reduce the cost to more acceptable levels (Figure 5.5). The advantage of such a plan is that it will be more appealing to

RAND*MR171-5.4*

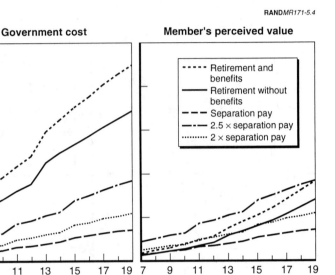

Figure 5.4—Comparison of Lump-Sum Options

RAND*MR171-5.5*

- Delay the start of the annuity

- Reduce the COLA

- Reduce the amount of the annuity (for those serving less than 20 years)

Figure 5.5—Further Options for Reducing Costs and Value of Early
Retirement Annuities

members closer to retirement, and it meets one of the political objectives by being consistent with the current retirement plan.

The cost of an early retirement annuity might be reduced to acceptable levels in three ways. The first is to delay the start of the annuity.

There is no legal requirement to begin the annuity at separation. ERISA does not establish a comparable requirement in the civilian community. Most private sector retirement programs do not initiate annuity payments until the employee is at least age 60. The second way to reduce the cost of the annuities is to reduce or eliminate the COLA protection. The final way to reduce the costs is to reduce the annuity payment by an amount proportional to the number of remaining years to regular retirement. This plan would probably appear equitable to members, since they entered the service expecting to serve 20 years to qualify for a retirement annuity. Reducing the annuity for leaving earlier is common in the civilian sector and could easily be explained to service members.

Figure 5.6 compares the present values of alternative plans that delay annuities until age 40 and age 62, respectively. From the government viewpoint, the cost of the age 40 annuity almost matches the retirement benefit at YOS 19 and is somewhat less for fewer YOS. The annuity at age 62 falls somewhat below separation pay. From the member's viewpoint, the values range from somewhat under

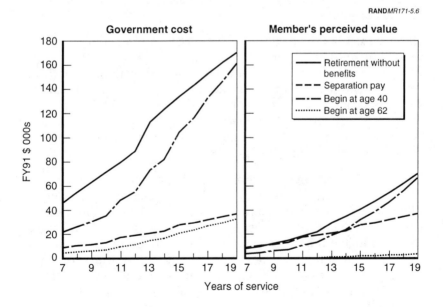

Figure 5.6—Delaying the Start of the Annuity

expected retirement to almost zero. The assumed discount rates for individuals of 12 percent imply that an annuity delayed until age 62 has a negligible present monetary value to the individual.

Delaying annuities provides a wide range of possibility for adjusting the value of early vesting plans. Although the calculations show that deferred annuities appear to be much more costly to the government than the perceived value to the individual, it is important to note two features of these alternatives. First, the political criterion of no regret is better solved by providing some deferred annuities. Lump sums that could be spent immediately could bring more long-term regret than deferred annuities. Thus, it may have a political value independent of any disadvantageous economic rationale. Second, individuals or their spouses may place a higher value on deferred annuities that begin at "normal" retirement age than we might expect by applying short-term discount rates. Indeed, individuals often make economic choices that seek to "protect themselves against themselves." Thus, overwithholding of taxes, Christmas club accounts, and other activities have the feature of being contrary to normal present value calculations but offer some security against current excessive consumption.

Next we examine the results of reducing COLA protection in an early retirement annuity (Figure 5.7). We compare an annuity that is fully COLA protected to one with reduced COLA protection. Specifically, we consider one that would subtract 1 percent from the annual consumer price index (CPI), as is currently done in the REDUX version of military retirement implemented in FY86. We also look at annuity payments without COLA protection. Again, nonmonetary retirement benefits are ignored in this comparison.

Reducing COLAs provides a more limited range of government costs than the previous option of deferring the annuity to age 62. Eliminating COLAs reduces the government costs by about 40 percent. From the member's viewpoint, reducing the COLAs still makes this offer higher than staying until retirement. Completely eliminating the COLA makes the offer almost equivalent to the expected retirement annuity. Adjusting COLAs appears to offer a much smaller cost reduction to the government compared to deferring the start of the annuity.

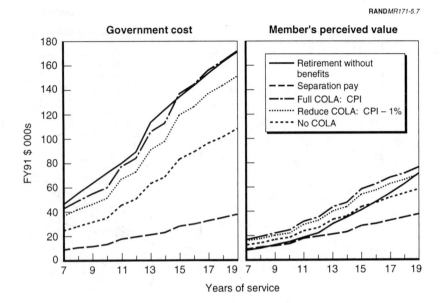

Figure 5.7—Reducing COLAs

We next compare the effects of reducing the initial payment in the annuity as a "penalty" to the individual for serving less than 20 years. For example, reducing the initial amount by 1 percent for each year less than 20 results in costs and perceived values reported in Figure 5.8. Under the current rule, an individual with 16 YOS who would have received 2.5 percent x 16 YOS x final pay = 40 percent of final pay would now receive a 1 percent penalty for each of the four years under 20 not served. Thus, under this scheme, the initial annuity payment would be 36 percent of final pay. We have also included the results obtained when the penalty is 1.5 percent and 2 percent, respectively. Since these formulas can result in payments lower than involuntary separation pay for fewer years of service, we have assumed that everyone would receive at least the current level of separation pay if they were involuntarily separated. Again, we omitted nonmonetary retirement benefits.

RAND*MR171-5.8*

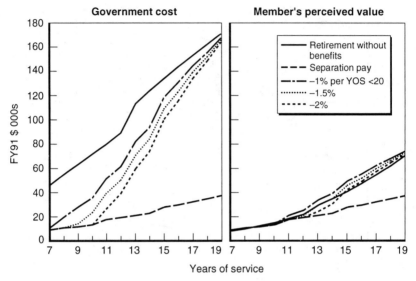

Figure 5.8—Reducing Payment for Those Serving Less Than 20 Years

These plans reduce the costs compared to the expected value of retirement. For those close to retirement, the penalty plans are only slightly less costly to the government than current retirement. However, for fewer YOS the cost saving increases. From the member's viewpoint, the plans are very close to the value of current retirement for all YOS. These plans appear to have the advantage of appealing to the entire 7–19 YOS range and reducing the government costs for all YOS.

At the same time, these plans may appear equitable to service members. All service members entered service with the expectation of having to serve 20 years before qualifying for a retirement annuity. Any plan that would provide an option for earlier retirement is unexpected, and members may feel that a penalty for not serving the full 20 years is fair.

Now we will examine several different hybrid plans that consist of an initial lump-sum payment with a deferred annuity.[2] Adding a long-term annuity to a lump-sum payment still allows taking partial advantage of the fact that lump sums provide the best "value" to the government, but this addition also addresses the long-term regret issue by providing a permanent retirement annuity. Such hybrid plans may also aid in achieving a consensus among OSD, the Army, and the Air Force. The Air Force favors a lump-sum plan, and the Army favors early retirement type plans. These hybrid offers combine features of both. The hybrid plans also combine two existing military compensation features, retirement and separation pay, and thus are consistent with the existing system. Finally, hybrid plans are sufficiently flexible to allow offers to be fine tuned, e.g., an offer designed to attract 20 percent of the target pool at early YOS and 50 percent at senior YOS (see Figure 5.9).

We present in Figure 5.10 two hybrid lump-sum/annuity plans to show the effect of starting annuities at different ages. Under the first plan, an individual with 19 YOS would receive a lump sum equal to involuntary separation pay and would begin to receive an annuity at age 40, but an individual with 7 YOS would begin an annuity at age

RAND*MR171-5.9*

- Develop contingency plans

- Seek service/OSD consensus

- React to potential Congressional changes

- Be consistent with current compensation system
    - Lump-sum separation
    - Longer-term annuity

Figure 5.9—Reasons for Considering Hybrid Plans

_____

[2]Asch and Warner (1994) also suggest that hybrid plans are desirable for incorporation as a basic element of the retirement system.

RANDMR471-5.10

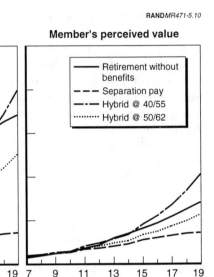

Figure 5.10—Examples of Hybrid Plans (without Benefits)

55. The second plan pictured here begins an annuity at age 50 for those with 19 YOS and at 62 for those with 7 YOS. We again omit benefits in these calculations.

The figures show that for senior members, the annuity must be moved back to around 45–50 years of age to provide perceived value equivalent to the retirement annuity. Starting an annuity earlier and providing a separation payment would provide a value greater than current retirement. For more junior members, annuities starting between 55–62 and a separation payment are equivalent in value to the current expected retirement annuity.

Plans could be shaped to produce any desired value using the parameters of the starting age of the annuity by YOS and the amount of the lump sum.

Figure 5.11 compares the same two hybrid plans but includes the value of military benefits. We value benefits at $3000 per year as discussed above, but only when the annuity is in effect. Thus, a military

RAND*MR171-5.11*

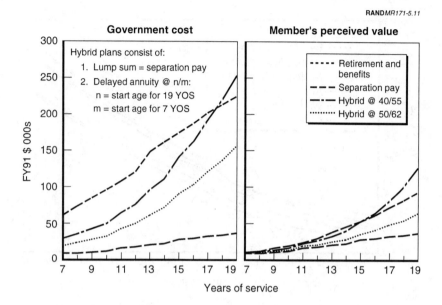

Figure 5.11—Examples of Hybrid Plans (with Benefits)

member who accepts the plan with 7 YOS at age 27 receives no benefits until his annuity starts at age 55 or 62, depending on which options were in effect.

We find that the relative attractiveness of hybrid plans, to either the government or the member, is about the same whether or not benefits are taken into account.

The present value calculations shown in Figure 5.12 are sensitive to a number of assumptions about how a member values various separation plans. Here we examine the effect of alternative assumptions. We begin with the same baseline condition that we have used throughout. The line labeled "No benefits, 12% rate" shows the present value of the monetary payment stream associated with the retirement package with a 12 percent discount rate as viewed by an Army enlisted person who plans to retire at 20 YOS as an E-6 and who regards his or her chances of reaching retirement as average. The value of benefits is omitted in this calculation.

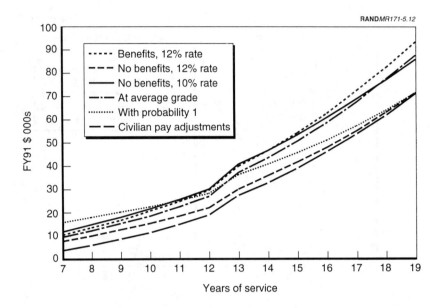

RAND*MR171-5.12*

Figure 5.12—Variations in Member's Perceived Value of Existing Retirement Plan

The line labeled "Benefits, 12% rate" differs in that it places a value of $3000 per year on the nonmonetary retirement benefits. The line labeled "No benefits, 10% rate" differs from the base case in that members are assumed to have a 10 percent discount rate, e.g., they discount the future less and value the retirement package more. As it turns out, this change in discount rates is almost equivalent to the addition of benefits.

The next case, denoted by a line labeled "At average grade," returns to the 12 percent discount rate and assumes that the individual expects to retire at the average grade at 20 YOS rather than at E-6. This assumption increases the final pay parameter by about 25 percent, which yields a corresponding increase in the monetary value of his retirement package. This also makes a difference almost equivalent to the change from 12 to 10 percent discount rate.

The last case, denoted by a line labeled "With probability 1," is identical to the base case in every respect except that the individual perceives that he will certainly stay until retirement, e.g., with probability one. This case makes little difference for senior personnel who already have high probabilities of retirement, but it changes the value for more junior members significantly. Some members who are planning on leaving or who think they will be involuntarily separated will have low probabilities of reaching retirement. Separation offers will look much more valuable to them than to those who judge their probability of reaching retirement to be high. However, the uncertainty caused by the drawdown may have affected nearly all younger members' perception of reaching retirement and would make separation offers very attractive. For these reasons, acceptance rates of offers to these younger members are more uncertain, and we need surveys or experiments to obtain improved estimates.

Finally, we have ignored civilian and military wages in our calculations. This is equivalent to assuming that the present values of the wage streams are equivalent regardless of when an individual leaves. Members who leave early for the civilian sector should make higher civilian wages in the long term because of their greater civilian experience. However, research has shown that civilian wages of military retirees tend to drop below their military wage initially, but retirees gradually obtain parity with their civilian peers.

Thus, members leaving early will probably earn less in the short term than if they had not separated but will earn more in the long run and more overall than if they had separated later. These two effects go in opposite directions and would partially cancel out the effects from not including wages in the calculations. This implies that the calculations may not be as sensitive to civilian wages as are other parameters. However, evidence indicates a net overall civilian income gain from leaving early, so some bias will remain.

Here we have taken into account one civilian pay variation to attempt to determine the sensitivity to civilian wage assumptions. We have assumed that military retirees take slight pay reductions of 15 percent when they initially enter the civilian work force but recover the difference and start earning 5 percent more than their military counterparts in about five years and earn 5 percent more in civilian earnings until retirement. Thus, the separatee would recover the difference in pay streams sooner and thus would value his military retirement less. It makes only modest differences in the present value of future income.

In summary, the most sensitive assumptions are the valuation of benefits, the discount rate, and the expected pay grade at retirement. For younger members, probability of reaching retirement can also change the valuation significantly.

Chapter Six

VOLUNTARY ACCEPTANCE RATES

METHODOLOGY

We will now estimate acceptance rates for different plans. The government should want to make the minimum offer that will yield the desired number of separations distributed over the force to provide the desired experience mix after the drawdown. Therefore, the services have to estimate not only the total number of voluntary separations each plan will produce, but how each plan will provide the desired skill and YOS profile. Further, since offers will be voluntary, the desired number separating must be obtained from offers made to a wider target group, and these target groups must be identified. In this chapter, we present a methodology for estimating target acceptance rates for each group for a set of Army plans. We use only the Army, since that is the only service to have developed detailed plans for how such offers would be made.

We begin this acceptance-rate analysis by presenting the methodology based upon the analysis scheme shown above (see Figure 6.1). We define acceptance rate as the percentage of individuals who would accept an offer from the population of individuals who would stay without an offer. We have used this definition of acceptance because it relates directly to defining the number of additional drawdown losses, and attracting these additional losses is the purpose of separation incentives. This acceptance rate will differ from the observed acceptance rate, since it includes both normal and drawdown losses. We will relate these two concepts below.

RAND*MR171-6.1*

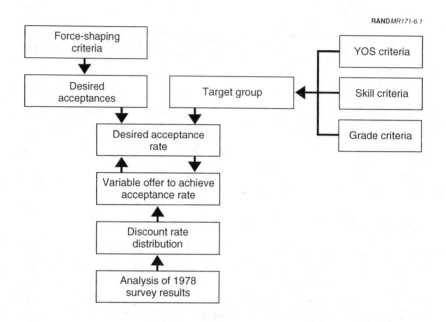

Figure 6.1—Schematic of Analysis Plan

The number of required separations is determined by force-shaping criteria with the steady-state template discussed above. Skill and quality target groups are then identified. For instance, the Army may decide that 28,000 additional separations are required and target those who have not been promoted to a given grade at a given YOS. These two parameters would define the needed target group acceptance rate. Of course, if the Army were willing to have a larger target group, a smaller acceptance rate would be required. However, offering a separation package to more would risk loss of higher-quality personnel. So, carefully limiting separation offers to those with lower skills is desirable from a force-quality perspective.

Having established target group goals, we next estimate acceptance rates for a given offer. First, we take a distribution of discount rates from data taken from the 1978 survey of military personnel (Black, 1983; Doering and Hutzler, 1982). We then use a simple rule to determine the discount rate at which a member would be indifferent to accepting a given offer or staying until retirement. This so-called breakeven discount rate[1] is then used together with the discount-rate distribution to determine the proportion of individuals in a given target group with discount rates greater than the breakeven discount rate. This number is the acceptance rate.

All individuals must decide between accepting a separation offer or continuing in the military with some expectation of reaching retirement (see Figure 6.2). We assume that an individual makes this decision by comparing the present value of the income streams generated by each choice. The first is equal to the accepted separation plan offer and the anticipated civilian income that would occur after separation. The second consists of the projected military pay including retirement payments plus any subsequent civilian pay. Both streams have uncertainties associated with estimating the present value. Key uncertainties are the pay grade achieved at 20 YOS, the level of future pay increases, and the probability of actually staying until 20 YOS. Civilian income streams now and in the future also are uncertain.

RAND*MR171-6.2*

- Relative attractiveness of compensation streams
  - Separation pay and civilian stream starting now
  - Military pay stream (current and possible retirement) plus future civilian stream
    - Uncertainty of military promotions and pay increases
    - Uncertainty of staying until retirement
      - Due to tenure rules
      - Due to drawdown
      - Due to future choices to stay
    - Uncertainty in future civilian opportunities
- Value of benefits
- Nonpecuniary considerations

Figure 6.2—Individual Criteria for Evaluation of Offer to Separate
Voluntarily

---

[1]This concept is similar to the internal rate of return calculated by firms when making decisions on capital expenditures. All capital projects are accepted when their estimated rate of return is higher than current market rates of return.

Younger people face greater uncertainty about reaching retirement as a result of the possibility of being involuntary separated because of tenure rules or drawdown policies and the possibility that they might leave the military voluntarily before retirement.

Benefits are an important part of the military retirement package and will also be valued differently by different people. Finally, nonpecuniary considerations, such as next assignments or spouse preferences, will also influence which plan is chosen.

To illustrate the decision a member faces, we show in Figure 6.3 the expected military pay streams associated with staying or leaving for an E-5 in YOS 13. The pay streams are given in real dollars for non-transferable VSI with and without COLAs, for regular retirement, and for regular retirement with benefits valued at $3000 per year. The pay stream starts immediately for those accepting the offer. The initial annual VSI annuity is determined by the current retirement rule.

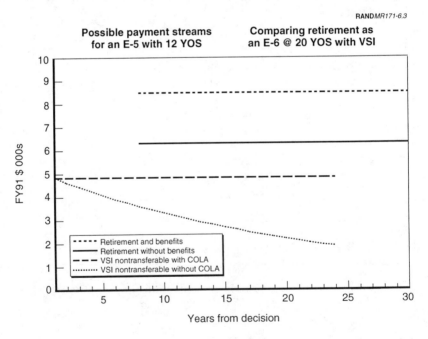

Figure 6.3—Comparing Expected Payment Streams Determines Breakeven Discount Rates

For those staying, the pay stream starts eight years later, and, according to the current retirement rule, equals 0.025 x 20 x base pay. For reference, we show what benefits would do to the retirement stream and what COLAs would do to the VSI stream.

The difference in the pay streams is that acceptance of one of the separation plans results in eight additional payments in the first eight years but a lower annual annuity and earlier termination of payments. The resulting present value will be greater if the additional payments are large enough to make up for the lower lifetime annuity. Moreover, since each plan is a different stream, there will be some discount rate at which the individual will be indifferent to the offers, i.e., the present value of the pay streams will be equal. We refer to this as the "breakeven" discount rate. This will generally vary by YOS and, of course, the specific separation offer made.

Figure 6.4 compares the breakeven discount rate associated with the COLA and non-COLA VSI offers to the regular retirement plus benefit stream. For individuals at 12 years of service, the breakeven discount

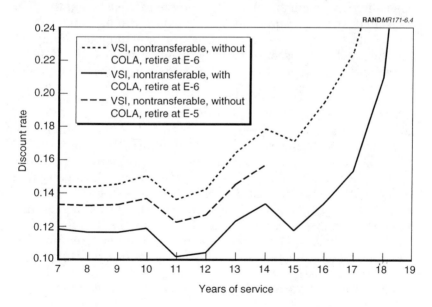

Figure 6.4—Breakeven Discount Rates Required to Equate Retirement
Payment Stream with VSI

rate for the COLA VSI is around 11 percent; it is 15 percent for the non-COLA VSI. According to our methodology, with a discount rate above 11 percent an individual would accept the COLA VSI, and with a discount rate above 15 percent an individual would accept the non-COLA offer. Given a distribution of discount rates for enlisted personnel by YOS, we can calculate the acceptance rate.

The rapid rise in discount rates for those close to retirement reflects the fact that there are fewer extra payments to make up for the loss of benefits and COLAs (in the non-COLA case). Essentially, individuals close to retirement would not accept the VSI offers because the one or two extra payments cannot make up for the loss of the value of retirement benefits not received.

The breakeven discount rate will depend on whether the individual expects promotion before retirement. The calculations shown here assume an individual on a "slow track." This individual achieved E-5 at 11 YOS and E-6 at 15 YOS. For individuals expecting higher pay grades and faster promotions, the breakeven discount rates for the same offer will be much higher. This difference means that the offer associated with a voluntary separation policy can be tuned to partially control the quality of those accepting by setting the amount so that the breakeven discount rate will be below the discount rate for those not expecting promotion but above the discount rate for those expecting promotion.

Figure 6.5 illustrates how we determine the acceptance rate for a specific offer given the breakeven discount rate of that offer and the distribution of discount rates for that cohort. We compute the breakeven discount rate that makes the offer's present value exactly equal to the present value of the expected retirement compensation for that cohort. We then assume that the offer will be accepted by the percentage of the members who have discount rates higher than the breakeven discount rate. Thus, for a given distribution of discount rates, the proportion of takers in the cohort is determined by the proportion of the area under the distribution curve lying to the right of the vertical line through the breakeven discount rate. In this example, we compute an offer using a 12 percent discount rate (the dashed line).

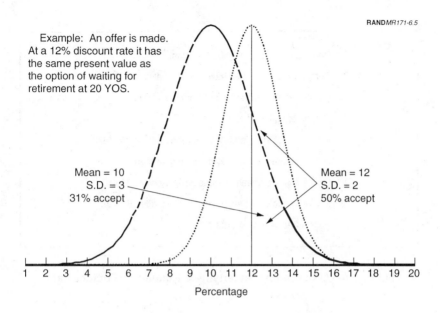

Example: An offer is made. At a 12% discount rate it has the same present value as the option of waiting for retirement at 20 YOS.

RAND*MR171-6.5*

Mean = 10
S.D. = 3
31% accept

Mean = 12
S.D. = 2
50% accept

Percentage

Figure 6.5—The Acceptance Rate Is the Area to the Right of the Corresponding Discount Rate

We can also work the problem backward to determine the offer required to obtain a desired acceptance rate from a given target group. If we want an acceptance rate of 31 percent of the Army E-5s with 16 years of service, for example, we would determine the discount rate required to ensure that 31 percent of the area under the curve lies to the right of that discount rate. The area to the right of the solid vertical line on the dotted normal curve represents 31 percent of the cohort. The present value of the required offer would be known because it is the value of retirement, discounted at the discount rate just determined. We would then tailor an offer to yield that present value, whether lump sum or an income stream discounted at the above determined rate or a hybrid.

A number of assumptions are required to apply the methodology to specific offers. These are listed in Figure 6.6. Most of these assumptions were discussed above. Below, we will examine the sensitivity of the acceptance rate to changes in these assumptions.

RAND*MR171-6.6*

1. Benefits are valued at $3000 per year.

2. Personal discount rates have a normal distribution.

3. Discount-rate parameters are from the literature.

4. Retirement grade is E-6.

5. Probability of reaching retirement is average for YOS.

6. Decisions are predicted by comparing present values.

7. Civilian income stream matches military until 20 YOS.

8. No difference in civilian income streams after 20 YOS.

9. Enlisted Army data are used.

Figure 6.6—Assumptions Underlying Estimated Acceptance Rates

We discuss our assumptions about discount rates in Figure 6.7. Our calculations assume that military pay is the average pay of all individuals present in a YOS and that retirement pay at 20 YOS is based on the pay of an E-6. We determine the rules for retirement pay based on when the individual entered the military. Three different retirement rules are currently used, depending on whether an individual entered military service before a specific date in FY80, between that date and a date in FY86, or after that date in FY86. (See the appendix for a more detailed description of the three rules.)

Assumptions 7 and 8 essentially mean that we assume no differences in annual earnings whether an individual leaves or stays in the military. If the individual leaves before 20 YOS, we assume that his civilian earnings match the military pay he would have received had he stayed. We also assume that civilian earnings after 20 YOS are the same regardless of when an individual left the military. Below, we make a more specific assumption that civilian earnings for early leavers fall 15 percent below military earnings initially but recover in 5 years and that civilian earnings of those leaving early will exceed by 5 percent those leaving at 20 YOS.

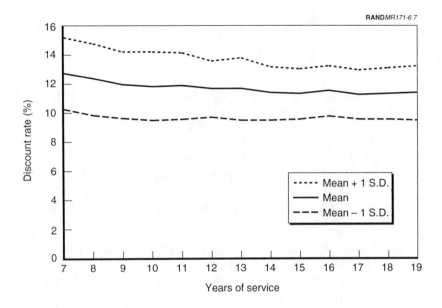

Figure 6.7—Discount Rates by Years of Service

The discount rates assumed here were taken from Black (1983) and are based on a survey of military personnel conducted in FY79 (Doering and Hutzler, 1982). Daula and Moffitt (1992) also estimate a real discount rate for enlisted personnel between their first and second terms of 11 percent, which is similar to Black's 12 percent. Although standard deviations of approximately 1 percent are calculated in Black, they are acknowledged not to reflect all sources of uncertainty. Their standard deviation takes account of differences due to the demographic mix of military personnel but does not reflect heterogeneous factors within demographic groups. Daula and Moffitt estimate a mean and standard error of 11 ± 4. Below, we present sensitivity analysis on this parameter; however, for these calculations we have doubled the reference's standard deviations reported by Black, which places us approximately midway between the value of Daula and Moffitt and the value of Black. It also tends to confirm the importance of the perceived probability of reaching retirement and to suggest that benefits are not valued very much in the initial reaction to an offer.

The values used for the means of these distributions are consistent with other estimates of discount rates taken from Navy reenlistment data (Cylke et al., 1982), and they are also confirmed by independent research (Landsberger, 1971).

Another important factor in analyzing voluntary acceptance patterns is how service members perceived the likelihood of reaching retirement. Figure 6.8 shows recent experience from cohort data from 1973 to 1990 for the proportion who reach retirement from a given YOS for the Army and the Air Force. There will be greater differences in assessed likelihood for more junior members, since some may be planning on leaving voluntarily, whereas others may be certain of staying and receiving the required promotions to escape involuntary separations due to tenure rules.

If the turmoil created by the existing drawdown and potential future deeper cuts drive the perceived likelihood of reaching retirement significantly lower than these figures, individuals will be more likely to accept an offer associated with a voluntary separation policy.

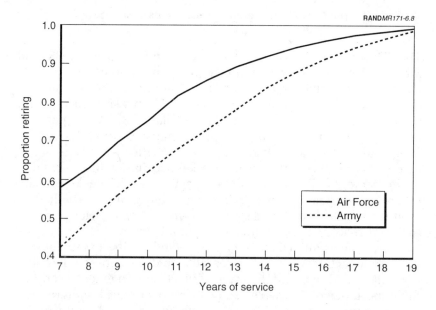

Figure 6.8—Proportion Retiring after Reaching YOS Indicated

DEFINING TARGET GROUPS

We will now define the potential target groups for an offer with a voluntary separation policy.

The target groups are defined by YOS, grade, and occupation. The Army identified specific groups to which it plans to offer some separation options (see Figure 6.9). The Army wants to separate between 25,000 and 35,000 lower-skill E-4s, E-5s, and possibly some E-6s, with between 8 and 16 YOS.

The Air Force has the largest deviation from the steady-state force structure, and between 15,000 and 22,000 need to be separated to maintain a balanced personnel structure. We assume these numbers for our analysis. The Navy and Marine Corps need to cut a smaller number of people than either the Army or the Air Force, unless further drawdowns are required.

The following figures show the size of the various separation target groups. In general, we suggest that the services target individuals in the lower pay grades at a given YOS and those with occupations with low replacement costs. Figure 6.10 compares the Army and Air Force

RAND*MR171-6.9*

- Army plans largest number of career separations
  - 25,000/35,000 desired
  - Specific plans formulated
    - 8–16 YOS
    - E-4, E-5, and E-6
    - Lower skill
  - Voluntary plans would avoid minority issues

- Air Force has most severe force-shaping problem
  - 15,000/22,000 desired separations

- Navy and Marine Corps have minimal requirements (with current drawdown levels)

Figure 6.9—Managing the Voluntary Enlisted Drawdown

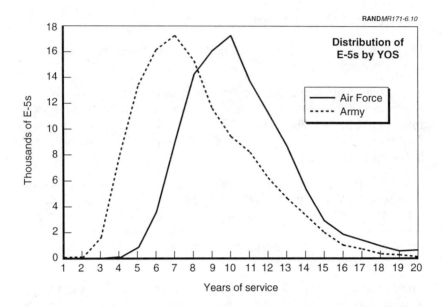

Figure 6.10—Both Services Have a Substantial Number of Senior E-5s with a Slow Promotion History

distributions of personnel in grade E-5. We recommend that they target for separation the more senior E-5s.

Figure 6.11 shows the Army distributions for E-4 through E-7 and the existing YOS retention control points (RCPs). E-4 "promotable," those selected but not yet promoted, denoted by E-4(P) by the Army, have traditionally been treated like E-5s for retention control purposes. E-5(P)s have been treated like E-6s. To facilitate the drawdown, the Army attempted to change the retention control point for E-4(P)s to the 8 YOS point, corresponding to the E-4 RCP, and to move the E-5(P) RCP to the 15 YOS point. However, this proposal led to the Congressional mandate restricting involuntary separations. Generally, the Army has chosen to target the senior promotable E-4s and E-5s, as well as some additional E-6s.

We show the same distributions for the Air Force, which recently implemented their first pre-20 YOS high year of tenure, or retention control rule, for E-4s at the 10 YOS point. A major point to be made

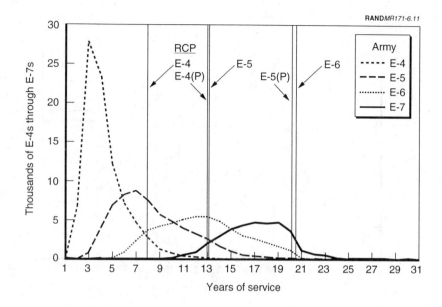

Figure 6.11—Army Should Target Members with Slow Promotion History

from Figures 6.11 and 6.12 is that both the Army and Air Force have large numbers of middle grade (E-4 through E-6) personnel who have progressed slowly in grade and are very senior in terms of years of service. These personnel would form the major portion of any target group for a policy of voluntary senior separations.

An additional consideration for defining the target group for any voluntary separation policy is occupation. In Figure 6.13, we have divided the military occupational codes into high, medium, and low technical skill levels. The services may not want to give people with high technical or critical skills the option of leaving early because of high replacement costs.   .

Figure 6.14 shows the Army distribution of E-5s by YOS divided into the three technical/occupational levels defined in Figure 6.13. Surprisingly, the low technical skill groups have about the same distribution as the other two groups. The Army's low technical skill group is nearly equal to the other two groups combined, at most years of service. There remains a large target group for voluntary

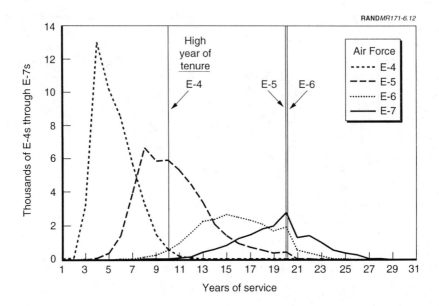

Figure 6.12—Air Force Should Also Target Members with Slow Promotion History

RAND*MR171-6.13*

- High technical level
  - Electronic equipment repairers
  - Communications and intelligence specialists
  - Medical and dental specialists

- Medium technical level
  - Electronic/mechanical equipment repairers
  - Other technical and allied specialists
  - Craftsmen

- Low technical level
  - Infantry, gun crews/sea specialists
  - Functional support and administration
  - Service and supply handlers

Figure 6.13—Technical Levels Assigned to Military Occupational Codes for this Analysis

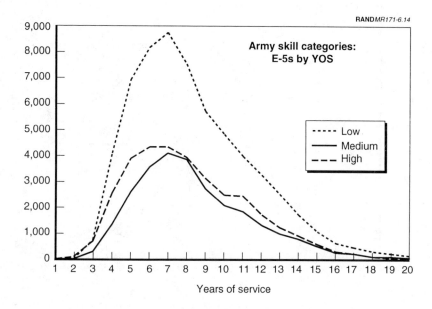

RAND*MR171-6.14*

Figure 6.14—Army Has a Sizable Target Group of Low- and Medium-Skill Levels

separation policies even when occupational categories are considered.

Figure 6.15 shows the same technical/occupational-level breakdown of E-5s by YOS for the Air Force. Again, surprisingly, all three levels have about the same YOS distribution. In the Air Force, however, the mode falls at YOS 10 versus the Army's YOS 7. This would offer larger target groups, but the Air Force low technical skill E-5s are only one-third of the population versus the Army's one-half of the population. Again, an adequate-sized target group remains, even when occupational categories are taken into consideration.

We have assumed that the Army desires about 28,000 voluntary enlisted separations from the 7–19 YOS group during the drawdown. It has identified specific target groups to achieve these reductions (see Figure 6.16). The darker portion of the leftmost bar is the number of E-4(P)s the Army wishes to separate at 8 YOS or later. The light portion is the number of additional E-4(P)s who also meet the

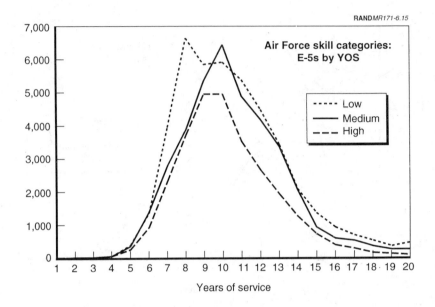

Figure 6.15—Air Force Also Has a Sizable Target Group of Low- and Medium-Skill Levels

desired criteria for separation. So the darker portion of the bar represents the acceptance rate required from the E-4(P) target group to achieve the number of separations required in FY92. An acceptance rate of about one-third is adequate to get a sufficient number of E-4(P)s in FY92 (about 5100).

The middle bar is E-5 promotables at 15 YOS, and the right bar is E-5 promotables and E-6s at 13 and 14 YOS. Rates of one-third and one-fourth would be required for these groups, respectively.

Figure 6.16 also shows the Army plan over the entire drawdown period. If the Army confines itself mainly to the E-4 and E-5 promotables, acceptance rates of one-half to two-thirds might be required; enlarging the group to E-5 promotables at 13 and 14 YOS makes the overall acceptance rates closer to one-third.

The key point here is that higher acceptance rates are required for the narrower target group, provided force shaping goals are met. Enlarging the group may mean losing somewhat higher quality

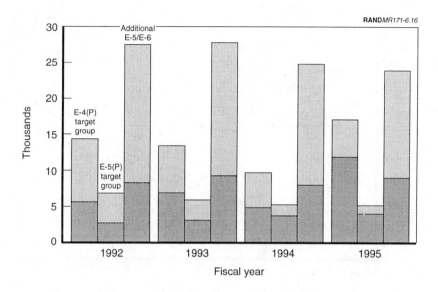

Figure 6.16—Comparing Target Groups with Separations Proposed in an
Army Plan—FY92–FY95

personnel, but it also means that the acceptance rate can decline
which—other things equal—may lower the offer.

ESTIMATING ACCEPTANCE RATES

We will now examine the results of the acceptance rate calculations
obtained using the assumptions and discount rate distributions just
discussed. These acceptance rates are all calculated assuming that
regular retirement with nonmonetary benefits valued at $3000 per
annum is the alternative to separating voluntarily.

Figure 6.17 shows the present value of an offer required to obtain a
given acceptance rate for each YOS. Acceptance rates of 90 percent
at 19 YOS would require a present value offer (lump sum) of
$120,000. For individuals at 7 YOS, 90 percent acceptances would be
obtained with offers of $22,000. The chart illustrates the sensitivity of
the acceptance rate to the value of the offer. For individuals at 19
YOS, acceptance rates go from 90 to 10 percent as offers range from
$120,000 to $80,000.

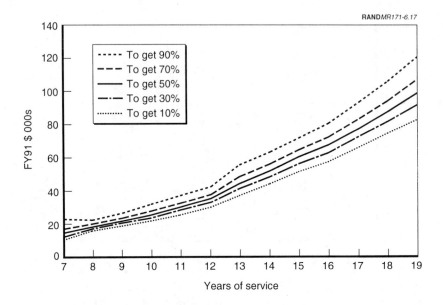

RANDMR171-6.17

Figure 6.17—Estimated Offer Required to Get a Given Acceptance Rate

Acceptance rates generally change rapidly over a narrow range of offers. Offers far below these ranges would be taken only by those who already plan on leaving.

We now present estimated acceptance rates for specific plans. Figure 6.18 shows the acceptance rate for nontransferable VSI without COLAs. The rates are approximately 20 percent at YOS 7, declining to near zero around YOS 16. VSI has low acceptance rates for senior personnel because the value of retirement benefits lost cannot be made up by the one or two extra payments that would be received before normal retirement. The scatter points illustrate that the calculation is done for each YOS separately, and they do not necessarily change in a linear fashion. The line is a least-square line fitted to the calculated acceptance rates by YOS.

Figure 6.19 shows the lines fit to estimated acceptance rates for six plans. These acceptance rates vary from essentially 100 percent for the early retirement option down to below 20 percent for the nontransferable VSI without COLA protection. Most plans show a strong

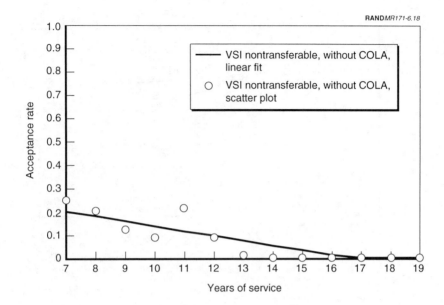

Figure 6.18—Estimated Acceptance Rates for VSI Base Case

dependence by YOS with higher rates for more junior personnel. This result partially occurs because of the absence of military benefits in any of the plans. In general, to shape the force correctly, the services need higher acceptances for senior than for junior personnel.

Most current plans appear to be directed at the wrong targets. An exception is the VSI transferable plan, which has a uniformly high acceptance rate of about 70–80 percent at all YOS. The hybrid plans mentioned above could be structured to yield any desired level with increasing rates by YOS. The "penalty plans" could also be structured for higher acceptance at more senior levels. These plans contain the flexibility to set both the level and slope of the acceptance rate line. Lump-sum plans, as well as nontransferable VSI plans, grow in amount nearly linearly with YOS and therefore decline in acceptance rate dramatically with YOS (since the value of retiring increases much more rapidly than does YOS).

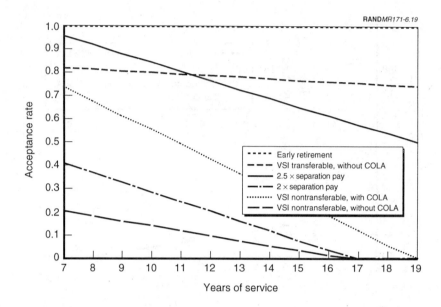

Figure 6.19—Proposed Plans Yield Widely Divergent Acceptance Rates

Figure 6.20 shows the sensitivity of acceptance rates to the expected pay grade at retirement. We show the acceptance rate for a VSI offer with COLA for two groups. The first group expects to retire at E-5 and the second group expects to retire at E-6. For more junior personnel, the differences in acceptance rates are very large. At 11 YOS, 60 percent of those expecting to retire at E-5 and 30 percent of those expecting promotion to E-6 would accept the offer. For senior personnel above 16 YOS, neither group would accept the offer.

This figure shows that the expected grade at promotion can produce different acceptance rates, but the acceptance rates are also sensitive to other factors.

Figure 6.21 examines the sensitivity of acceptance rates to five other factors: the value of benefits, an increase in discount rates of two percentage points, an increase in the standard deviation by one percentage point, retiring at the average pay at 20 YOS rather than the assumed E-6, and assigning a probability of one to reaching retirement.

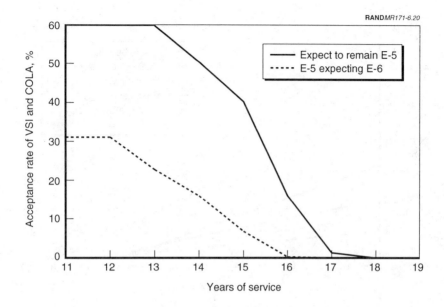

Figure 6.20—Voluntary Senior Separation Offers Could Be Designed to Control Who Accepts

Starting from a base case condition—the nontransferable VSI option without COLA protection—we see that the acceptance rates increase dramatically if the service member assigns no monetary value to the medical benefits and commissary and exchange privileges associated with the retirement package. Acceptance rates at 11 years of service would jump from 11 to 50 percent for such individuals.

This figure also indicates that our entire set of calculations is very sensitive to the mean and distribution of the valuation of benefits by military personnel. A change in the mean discount rate from 12 to 14 percent would also change acceptance rates markedly. At 11 YOS, the rates would climb from 11 to 33 percent; of course, we would see a marked decrease if our average discount rate were below 12 percent. Similarly, increasing the standard deviations used in the discount-rate distributions increases acceptance rates slightly because of increased differences in taste in the cohorts. We also see that when service members perceive that they will retire at the average pay grade for 20 YOS (rather than at E-6) or that they are certain to

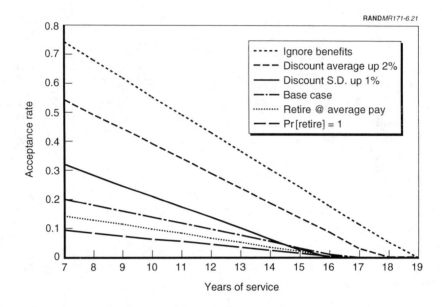

Figure 6.21—Sensitivity of Estimated Acceptance Rates

reach retirement, the expected value of retirement increases with a corresponding decrease in the likelihood of accepting any offer to separate voluntarily.

Sensitivity of acceptance to the perceived probability of reaching retirement is discussed further in Figure 6.22.

One factor that could drastically change acceptance rates for more junior personnel is changing their perception of reaching retirement because of changing personnel management policies during the drawdown. Figure 6.22 examines the sensitivity of acceptance rate to the uncertainty of reaching retirement. The base case reflects acceptance rates for the nontransferable VSI without COLAs for individuals who assume that they have an average chance of reaching retirement. The sensitivity analysis shows the acceptance rate if this probability varies from 0.25 of the average probability to a probability of one. Under the assumption of "25 percent of the average," the acceptance rates increase to one for all groups. Even if

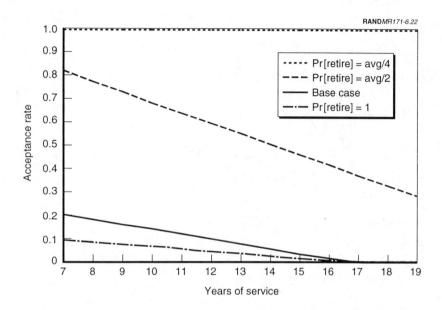

Figure 6.22—Sensitivity of Estimated Acceptance Rates to Member's
Perceived Retirement Probability

the assessed chances are one-half of the present average, acceptance
rates increase dramatically.

This assessment is likely to be a key factor in the decisions of younger
personnel, and thus estimating acceptance rates for this group is
somewhat perilous. If these members are convinced, or can be convinced (say by a "carrot and stick" approach) that even if they refuse
the offer the services will not let them reach retirement, then the
"voluntary" acceptance rate could be quite high.

Previous research and economic theory can help identify the characteristics of individuals more likely to accept voluntary separation offers (see Figure 6.23). As we saw in Figure 6.22, anyone who
perceives that the chances of reaching retirement are low will be
likely to value any offer more highly than a potential retirement
package. This group includes those who might have been planning
to leave anyway as well as those who feel they might be caught by a

RAND*MR171-6.23*

* Perceived lower probability of reaching retirement
    – Voluntary leavers
    – Tenure rule force-outs
    – Drawdown induced
* Perceived lower grade at retirement
* Higher discount rate
* Larger difference in civilian pay stream with respect to military pay stream
* Low value for military benefits (if not offered)
    – Smaller families
    – Low health costs
    – Likely health coverage in civilian jobs

Figure 6.23—Characteristics of Likely Takers

retention control point, high-year-of-tenure rule, or involuntary separations during drawdown.

Those who expect promotion before retirement will be less likely to leave than those who do not, provided civilian opportunities are equivalent. However, civilian opportunities may be greater for those experiencing faster promotion in the military, making the civilian pay differences important in their decisions. It is important to realize that it is the relative difference in expected military and civilian pay streams that affects separation decisions. This relative difference means that one cannot simply say that those with higher civilian offers will be more likely to leave. Individuals who receive high civilian offers may also be more likely to have higher military pay expectations because of faster promotion.

Those with higher discount rates would be more likely to accept an offer. Previous research supports the hypothesis that discount rates decrease with YOS, level of skill training, and years of education (Black, 1983) so that—other things equal—those with less experience and education and lower skills would be more likely to accept. Discount rates are also higher for minority groups.

Finally, if offers do not include benefits, those who would place a low value on the nonmonetary retirement benefits have a higher likelihood of accepting. These groups include those with few dependents or little perceived requirement for medical care as well as those who might anticipate that civilian employment would cover medical needs after separation.

We have previously defined acceptance rate as an analytic concept that is the rate of acceptances among those who would not normally have left during the year of the offer. We refer to those who would have left anyway as normal losses and to those who leave because of new policies as drawdown losses. This acceptance rate cannot be observed directly, since we cannot distinguish in a target group between the normal and drawdown losses. Rather, the observed number of acceptances is the sum of normal and drawdown losses.

We have used the analytic definition of acceptance because it relates directly to defining the number of drawdown losses, and attracting drawdown losses is the purpose of separation incentives. Thus, the amount of an offer must be directly related to this analytic acceptance rate. On the other hand, the observed acceptance rate determines the number of actual acceptances and will determine the cost of the program. It also will be the only empirically observed parameter.

The relationship between the analytical rate and observed acceptance rate can be specified. If an offer is given to a target group, the analytic acceptance rate, A, is given by

$$A = D / (T - L)$$

and the observed acceptance rate is given by

$$OA = (D + L) / T$$

where

> D = drawdown losses,
> L = normal losses,
> T = number in target group (number of offers), and
> $C = (T - L) / T$ = normal continuation rate.

Using these two equations, the relationship between the two rates can be expressed in terms of the normal continuation rate, C.

$$A = (OA + C - 1)/C$$

In practice, the analytic acceptance will be estimated from the observed rate and an estimation of the normal continuation rate of the target group. The normal continuation rate must be estimated from historical data or through surveys given to those offered the incentive.

Figure 6.24 illustrates the relationship between the observed acceptance rate (OA) and the analytic acceptance rate (A) for different annual normal continuation rates. For continuation rates of one, there are no normal losses, and the two rates are equal (the line at 45 degrees on the graph). The rates diverge the most when normal losses

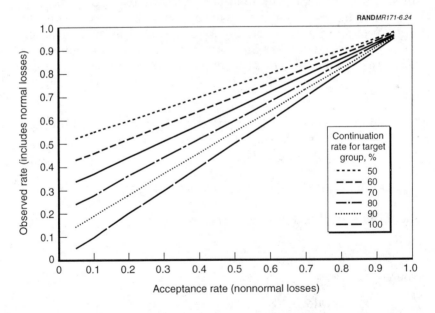

Figure 6.24—The Observed Acceptance Rate for Any Groups Will Include Normal Losses

are high and drawdown losses are low. This occurs for low continuation rates and low analytic acceptance rates. For a continuation
rate of 0.5, the observed rate of 0.6 will produce an analytic rate of
0.2.

Chapter Seven

MANAGING VOLUNTARY SEPARATION COSTS

The costs of separation offers will be a major determinant of their desirability and use by the services. There are several cost issues. First, accepted separation offers often replace future retirement payments and thus reduce the future military retirement liability. Any reasonable plan for early separation will result in net government savings. However, the separation outlays will probably occur before the savings from reduced retirement expenditures are realized. An important issue is how this reduced liability reflects in the DoD budget and how it might affect the DoD budget agreement ceiling.

A second related question is how the outlays are spread over time and from what account they should be paid. Separation payments in the form of annuities will have less immediate budgetary effect than lump-sum settlements. There is also the question of whether payments should be made from past contributions into the Treasury military retirement account (since that is where the long-term saving will be reflected) or from current DoD contributions to the retirement account.

Part of the cost issue involves addressing the efficient use of separation payments. Their purpose is to create voluntary losses over and above the usual rate of voluntary losses. However, the offer cannot be made only to those who would not have left if no offer was made. Some payments will go to individuals who would have left anyway. For any offer, there will also be individuals who would have been willing to leave at some lower offer. Economists define the concept of "economic rent" as the portion of payments that would be unnecessary if the flexibility existed to negotiate with each individual separately. It is the cost incurred by deciding for equity's sake to make a uniform offer to any group of individuals.

Here we will be concerned with only that part of the economic rent represented by payments to individuals who would have left even without an offer. We have some influence over how many individuals we pay by defining target groups by occupation, YOS, and grade. However, once such groups are defined, current policy dictates a uniform offer. We will thus focus on an efficiency measure that calculates the cost per drawdown loss, where the cost includes payments to both normal and drawdown losses.

The proportion of separation pay paid as economic rent to those who would have left without offers depends on the normal losses in a given year of service and on the acceptance rate (Figure 7.1). Higher annual loss rates mean that more "normal" separatees will be included in any offer made. For instance, if an offer is made to a representative target group, those planning on leaving will accept the

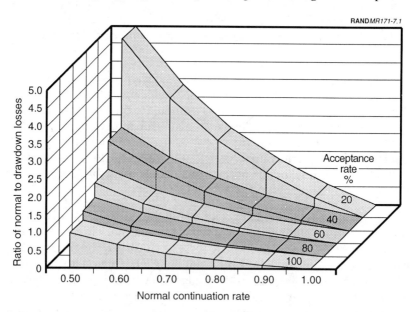

Figure 7.1—Economic Rent as a Function of Acceptance Rate and
Continuation Rate

offer and so will those attracted to leave solely because of the offer. Higher normal losses occur at lower YOS, thus, more economic rent will be paid for more junior personnel.

Economic rent will also depend on the amount of the offer. For example, an offer too low to attract any additional separatees will still be accepted by those already planning on leaving, and, in this case, the entire separation budget would be paid as economic rent. Thus, offers that are too low will be very inefficient. On the other hand, high offers that would attract everybody in a defined target group would also be inefficient because the marginal return in additional acceptances declines with offer size at high offer levels. This effect occurs in our theory because the discount rate of a given target group is assumed to be normally distributed, and for each increment of offer, fewer individuals will be willing to leave as acceptance rates approach one. A more complex case is presented when target groups differ in quality characteristics; this will be discussed below.

This figure shows rent expressed as the ratio of normal to drawdown losses among those receiving payments. It is shown as a function of acceptance rate and annual continuation rate. The simple formula is:

$$\text{Ratio} = (1 - C)/A$$

where

$$
\begin{aligned}
\text{ratio} &= \text{the ratio of normal to drawdown losses,} \\
C &= \text{the continuation proportion, and} \\
A &= \text{the analytical acceptance rate.}
\end{aligned}
$$

As both continuation and acceptance rates decline, the proportion of normal losses in the group accepting the offer increases. The higher the proportion of normal losses, the less efficient the offer. For the years of service between 7 and 19, annual continuation rates usually exceed 80 percent, so we have shown only the upper end of the continuation rate range. For continuation rates in the range above 80 percent, very little rent is paid as long as acceptance rates are above 20 percent. Offers yielding acceptance rates below 20 percent are very inefficient judging by our measure of normal to drawdown losses, because they include a larger portion of those who would leave anyway, and such offers should probably be boosted until they achieve higher acceptance rates. Figure 7.2 addresses this tradeoff.

We can calculate a measure of effectiveness for the offer as the total cost of accepted offers per drawdown loss. Although, as mentioned, the purpose of the offer is to produce drawdown losses, it will also be accepted by those who would have voluntarily left. Therefore, offers that produce more drawdown losses relative to voluntary losses in a given year of service will be more effective. A measure of this is the cost of the incentive per drawdown loss.

The outlay cost of the incentive is the total acceptances (voluntary losses + drawdown losses) times the amount of the offer. This calculation assumes that the normal loss rate at 13 YOS is 4.5 percent, and all of these individuals will of course accept any offer. We then assume that the rate of drawdown losses (acceptance rate) depends on the amount of the offer. Higher offers bring higher acceptance rates.

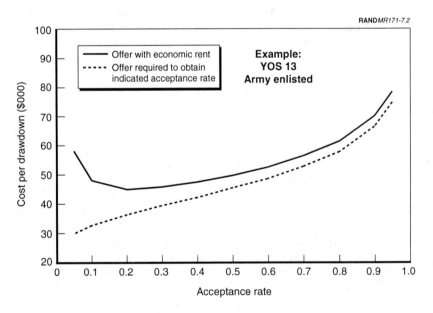

Figure 7.2—There is an "Optimal" Career Separation Offer for a Given Target Group

In general, the shape of the effectiveness curve as a function of acceptance rate (holding normal loss rate constant) must be U-shaped. Acceptance rates close to zero mean that only normal losses will receive payments, i.e., the cost per drawdown loss approaches infinity as the acceptance rate approaches zero. At the other extreme, when the acceptance rate approaches one, the cost/drawdown loss will also approach infinity, since the amount of the offer required to attract the last individual could be very high.

We first assume a fixed target group with a normally distributed discount rate with no quality distinctions among personnel. We estimate the costs per drawdown loss for different levels of offers made and the implied rates of acceptance produced. Under this scenario, the figure shows, for a 13 YOS group, the cost per drawdown loss as the acceptance rate (and size of the offer) is increased. The figure shows that for very small acceptance rates, the cost per drawdown will increase exponentially approaching infinity as the acceptance rate approaches zero (no drawdown losses). The figure shows that the level of offer is $30,000 for a 5 percent acceptance rate and the cost per drawdown loss would be approximately $60,000.

As the offer increases from $30,000 to $40,000, the acceptance rate increases from 5 to 30 percent, and the cost per drawdown declines to approximately $45,000 per drawdown loss. The approximate minimum cost per drawdown for this group occurs between 20 and 40 percent acceptance rate and is approximately $45,000 per drawdown loss. As the offer level and acceptance rate increase beyond this, the cost per drawdown increases until it reaches about $70,000 per drawdown loss at acceptance rates of 90 percent and offer levels of $67,000. This increase occurs because the normally distributed discount-rate distribution yields smaller and smaller increments of acceptance rates at the extremes of the discount-rate distribution.

If we assume that there are no quality differences in personnel at a given YOS and that we have no preference for who leaves, then this methodology can yield the size of offer and target group required to achieve a given number of drawdown losses while minimizing the cost per drawdown. Under our assumptions for YOS 13 (4.5 percent normal attrition), the offer sizes should be sufficient to achieve approximately 30 percent acceptance rates and the size of target groups to achieve a given number, N, of drawdown losses would be:

$$NT = ND /.30(1 - L)$$

where

$$
\begin{aligned}
NT &= \text{size of target population,} \\
ND &= \text{desired drawdown losses, and} \\
L &= \text{normal attrition rate.}
\end{aligned}
$$

If 5000 drawdown losses were desired for YOS 13 and normal attrition is 5 percent, then the size of the target population given the offer of $40,000 should be 17,500 to minimize the cost of the program. The program costs would be $40,000 times acceptances (5000 + .05 x 17,500) equals $240 million. It should be noted that the cost per drawdown increases slowly as acceptance rates increase from 30 to 50 percent. At 50 percent acceptance, the offer size is $47,000 and the costs of achieving 5000 drawdown losses would be $260 million— an increase of only $20 million. However, the size of the target group narrows significantly to 10,500.

A narrower target group has significant advantages if we loosen our assumption that all personnel are of equal quality. If, for instance, we could rank personnel in terms of quality characteristics, and could establish target groups starting from low quality, then it would be desirable to have more narrowly defined target groups focusing on lower-quality personnel. In this case, one must decide how much it is worth achieving higher acceptance rates by paying a higher cost per drawdown to leave higher-quality personnel in the force. For instance, in our example above, would paying $260 million to take more personnel out of a lower-quality group of 10,500 be better than paying $240 million but having slightly higher-quality personnel separate from the 17,500 target group?

Answering this question requires having good measures of the relative productivity of service personnel and also an understanding of how the distribution of discount rates and outside income opportunities changes for low- and high-quality personnel. In general, these parameters are not currently well defined, but more complex econometric analysis focusing on the decisions to leave could improve these estimates (see, for instance, Daula and Moffitt, 1992). However, if relative productivity profiles and distributions of discount rates and outside income were available for personnel of different productivity, then the methodology could be used to better define the optimal offers.

In the absence of better estimates, one should note that higher offers and higher acceptance rates (up to 0.60) add relatively small increments to costs, and if good military judgments can be made about the quality profile of target groups, then it is probably better to aim for acceptance rates of 40 to 60 percent rather than 20 to 40 percent. On the other hand, if the quality of personnel in the smaller and larger target groups is approximately the same, then acceptance rates of 20 to 40 percent should probably be the objective.

Figure 7.3 shows the effectiveness curves for different years of service using the specific natural attrition rate for each YOS as well as the

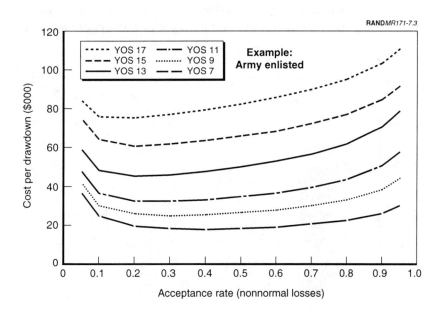

Figure 7.3—Acceptance Rates Between 20 Percent and 50 Percent
(Depending on YOS) Define Near-Optimal Offers

specific curve of acceptance rate as a function of offer level for each YOS derived from our analysis above. The cost per drawdown naturally rises by YOS because the expected retirement annuity rises. However, each YOS curve has a U-shaped profile and the strictly optimal acceptance rate moves slowly from about 20 percent for YOS 17 to somewhat higher values as YOS declines. The curves generally get flatter for lower YOS values, indicating that acceptance rates from 10 to 70 percent provide little difference in cost per drawdown.

This implies that if accurate quality judgments can be made about groups of military personnel, then acceptance rates as high as 70–80 percent would be efficient for lower YOS groups, whereas somewhat lower limits of around 50–60 percent could be set for higher YOS personnel.

Figure 7.4 shows initial cost estimates of a specific Army enlisted drawdown plan that requires 28,000 losses. Cost estimates are in terms of the present value of separation payments discounted at the assumed government real rate of 4 percent. Three plans are compared: early retirement, VSI without COLA, and 2.5 x separation pay.

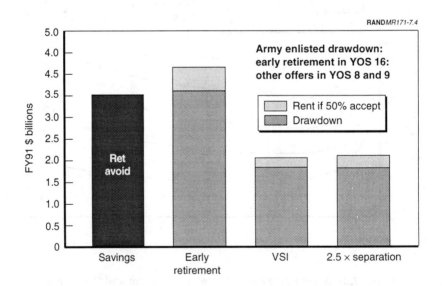

Figure 7.4—Costs of Separation Offers

It also estimates the present value of avoiding future retirement costs.

In making these estimates, we held constant the required number of drawdown losses and assumed that each plan achieves these losses with an acceptance rate of 50 percent. (In Figure 7.5, we will vary the acceptance rate for each plan.) We also assumed that each target group is a random draw from the Army enlisted force given a YOS. This assumption means that their continuation rate is average for that YOS. The cost is simply the number of acceptances times the present value of the particular offer. The number of acceptances is the 28,000 drawdown losses plus normal losses. Since we have assumed for this initial estimate that acceptance rates are the same across plans, then the number of normal losses will be the same across plans. The differences in cost estimates are thus driven entirely by the particular plan and the payment schedule. The figure shows that the early retirement option—as noted above—would be the most expensive and would actually cost more than the retirement avoidance. Outlay for the Army in present-value terms would be over $4 billion. The VSI and 2.5 x separation pay lump sum would cost about $2 billion and would net substantial long-term savings to the government.

Figure 7.5 shows how costs vary within a given plan at different acceptance rates. The figure first shows the estimated retirement costs avoided because of those accepting offers who would have later retired. It is approximately $3.5 billion. The figure then shows the costs of offering three different retirement plans: early retirement, VSI, and a lump sum equal to 2.5 x separation pay. Costs for each plan are calculated using four assumptions. The first assumes only the costs for drawdown losses; the remaining assumptions add the costs of normal losses. The three levels of normal losses assume acceptance rates of 90, 50, and 20 percent acceptance rates. Thus, each bar corresponding to a program shows the costs of drawdown losses and total costs if 90, 50, and 20 percent acceptance rates are achieved.

RAND*MR171-7.5*

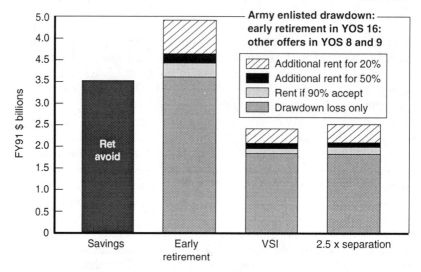

Figure 7.5—Comparison of Economic Rent Costs

The major determinant of costs is whether early retirement as opposed to either VSI or a lump sum is offered. However, acceptance rates are a secondary determinant of costs and costs grow as acceptance rates drop to around 20 percent or lower. This figure supports offers that achieve acceptance rates above 20 percent.

Figure 7.6 shows the actual outlays associated with three plans and illustrates one of the key tradeoffs. Plans that give lump-sum settlements are the most cost effective for the government because they take maximum advantage of the differences in discount rates between the government and individuals. However, lump-sum settlements maximize outlays in the short term, and they do not solve the problem of possible longer-term regret by the acceptor. This figure shows that the outlays over the drawdown period for a lump-sum settlement of 2.5 x separation pay would average about $450 million for the enlisted Army. On the other hand, VSI payments would be stretched over 20 or more years, would average only $100 million in the drawdown period, and would never exceed $200 million.

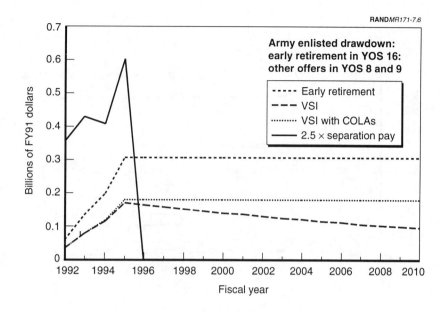

Figure 7.6—Total Outlay for Volunteer Separations

Figure 7.7 compares separation payments with the annual contributions to the military retirement fund (curve at the top of the chart). The Army will contribute between $2.8 billion and $3.5 billion annually to the fund over the next 15 years. Separation payments replace future retirement payments and reduce the future military retirement liability. As shown above, any reasonable plan for early separation will result in net government savings. However, the outlays for separation payments will probably occur before the retirement payments that are avoided. A method is needed to reflect in current budgets the net savings from the increased levels of voluntary separations.

The payments to the military accrual retirement system have been made without assuming a drawdown, and thus the fund will experience a large gain as a result of the higher than normal losses associated with the drawdown. These payments are made to the Treasury and reflect the annual accrued liability for future retirement obligations. Within the DoD budget, separation payments could be offset by reduced retirement contributions if the actuarial

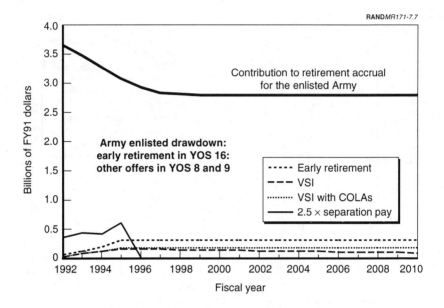

Figure 7.7—Outlays for Career Separations Should Be Offset by Adjusting Retirement Accrual Contributions

computations were made in a way that reflected the avoided retirement liability contemporaneously with the separation payment. In fact, the avoided liability from retirement will be greater than the separation payment.

However, this offset occurs only within the DoD budget and leaves a problem for deficit financing. The DoD contributions to the Treasury Military Retirement Fund are intergovernmental transfers requiring no new taxes nor do they affect the budget deficit. Separation payments, on the other hand, are new outlays. Although the DoD accrual contributions should decline to reflect lower liability, this decline will not offset the separation payments in terms of government outlays. Congress will have to appropriate additional money to pay for the separation payments, and DoD may have to offset the payments within a budget ceiling with dollars spent on other personnel costs, readiness, or procurement.

Another possibility is for the DoD budget ceiling to be adjusted to reflect the net savings from the drawdown separations. Thus, the ceilings could be adjusted upward to reflect the lower liability. Decisions would have to be made about the timing of the adjustments. One method would be to reflect the savings simultaneously with the separation outlays. Thus, lump-sum settlements would generate a higher DoD budget ceiling that would more than offset the separation payment. This would provide incentive to DoD to carry out the drawdown efficiently. However, unless the service budgets reflected their individual drawdown plans, the services themselves would have no monetary incentives.

Early separations will also reduce ordinary personnel costs, and these reductions will partially offset the separation costs. Figure 7.8 shows the personnel budget for the Army for a number of drawdown plans by fiscal year. The cuts will save approximately $2.5 billion. However, the magnitude of the savings depends on which drawdown

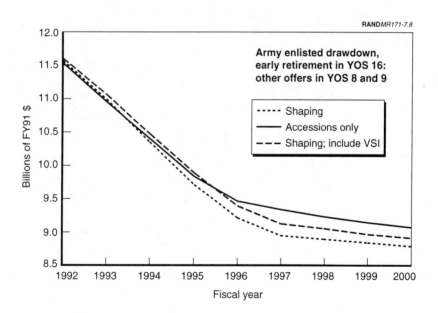

Figure 7.8—Voluntary Separations Bring About Reduced Pay and
Allowance Outlays

plan is implemented. The accession-only drawdown plan nets the least saving. The budget for the Army drawdown discussed previously is shown with and without the VSI payments included. For the VSI plan, which spreads payments over many years, the personnel costs savings from force reductions dominate the budgetary picture.

Chapter Eight

CONCLUSIONS

We draw the following conclusions based on this and previous analyses of the drawdown (Grissmer and Rostker, 1992) and summarized in Figures 8.1 to 8.4.

We have developed a methodology that allows estimation of the efficient size of voluntary separation offers required to meet drawdown loss requirements and the size of the associated target group receiving the offer for each YOS group. The initial assumptions we have made include a normally distributed discount rate for all military

RAND*MR171-8.1*

- Separation offers yielding drawdown acceptance rates of 10–50 percent (depending on YOS) are the most efficient
  - Avoids excessive economic rent
  - Avoids unnecessarily high offers
  - Avoids targeting high-quality groups
  - Provides effective force shaping
- Offers yielding higher acceptance rates at 13–18 YOS and lower rates at 7–12 YOS are desired
  - Higher acceptance rates needed at 13–18 YOS for force shaping
  - More man-years avoided at 13–18 YOS minimizing drawdown losses
  - Personnel savings and retirement avoidance larger for 13–18 YOS
  - Low-quality target groups more easily identified at 13–18 YOS
  - Less uncertainty in acceptance rates for 13–18 YOS

Figure 8.1—Determining Size of Offer and Target Groups to Minimize Budgetary Costs

RAND*MR171-8.2*

- No currently proposed plans yield 10–50 percent acceptance rates with higher rates for senior YOS
    - Early retirement has acceptance rates over 95 percent for all YOS
    - VSI plans
        - Transferable plan has acceptance rates too high (70–80 percent) at all YOS
        - Nontransferable without COLA has acceptance rates too low (0–20 percent) at senior YOS
        - Nontransferable with COLA has acceptance rates too high (50–70 percent) at junior YOS
    - Lump-sum payments
        - 2 × separation pay has acceptance rates too high (50–80 percent) at junior YOS
        - 2.5 × separation pay has acceptance rates too high (50–90 percent) for all YOS

Figure 8.2—Evaluation of Current Plans

RAND*MR171-8.3*

- Hybrid plans (lump-sum payment plus deferred annuity) can be easily structured to meet political, economic, and equity objectives simultaneously
    - Show similar structure to retirement annuity for very senior YOS
    - Show similar structure to separation pay for more junior YOS
    - Solve long-term regret problem with annuity
    - Take partial advantage of discount rate differences between government and individual with lump-sum payment
    - Fit comfortably within the current structure of military compensation
    - Shift a significant portion of costs to the military retirement fund
    - Contain elements of previous plans proposed by Army, Air Force, and OSD

Figure 8.3—Evaluation of Hybrid Plans

personnel and no quality preference among military personnel at a given YOS and no difference in external income opportunities within each YOS. Under these assumptions, the methodology defines an

RAND*MR171-8.4*

- All plans except early retirement result in significant net present value government savings
    - Budget agreements and future accrual contributions should reflect saving
    - Savings must be reflected in individual service budgets to create force shaping incentives
- Careful OSD and service management is essential
    - Large uncertainty in absolute (but not relative) acceptance rates
        - Uncertainty higher for more junior YOS
        - Early calibration and adjustment to absolute levels needed
        - Lump sum can provide adjustment mechanism
        - Must be designed initially to increase acceptance rates with YOS
    - Individual decisions on offers should be well informed and strictly voluntary
        - Accurate information about promotion, career expectations, and financial considerations should be available
        - "Carrot and stick" approach detrimental to longer-term interests

Figure 8.4—Cost Savings and Management

offer and acceptance rate that minimize the cost per drawdown loss for each YOS.

Under the assumptions made in this analysis, the acceptance rate range that produces minimum cost per drawdown is between 20 and 40 percent for the enlisted force between 7–19 YOS. However, the analysis shows that the costs per drawdown are fairly insensitive for all YOS groups up to 50–60 percent. Staying above 20 percent is necessary to avoid paying excessive economic rent, and staying below 70–80 percent will avoid unnecessarily high offers that bring few additional drawdown losses at the margin.

If we assume that accurate judgments of performance can be made among groups of personnel within each MOS, and target groups can be defined for different quality groups, then setting offers toward the high side of efficient acceptance rates will allow a much narrower targeting of offers and will result in a higher-quality force remaining after drawdown. This means acceptance rates of 50–60 percent for all YOS groups. Our analysis of target groups indicates that there will be sufficient personnel to meet drawdown objectives if those with lagging promotion rates are targeted.

Our analysis indicates that drawdown losses from the 7 to 19 YOS groups are desirable to maintain steady-state experience profiles over time. A somewhat higher proportion of personnel would be required among the more senior groups than among junior groups. Reductions in the more senior group will also ensure larger personnel cost savings and retirement avoidance savings, and will reduce the total number of personnel required to leave service. Since this senior group will require higher separation offers, programs structured for this group should be the cornerstone for designing the separation pay incentive.

Although we have established an efficient acceptance-rate range for each YOS group, the specific acceptance-rate target for the more senior group will depend on more detailed service information about occupation and grade requirements and the quality differentials within and between YOS groups. The services could prioritize target groups beginning with lower-quality and low occupational skill groups and gradually move to higher-quality groups. They could then begin offers with the highest-priority groups (low quality, low skill), determine acceptance rates, and gradually move to the lower-priority groups until force-shaping requirements are met.

Plans should probably be designed to hedge the uncertainty so that it is more likely to achieve higher than lower acceptance rates. Higher acceptance rates may imply some inefficiency but will still achieve force shaping and retirement avoidance, while ensuring that only lower-quality groups would need to be targeted. Acceptance rates that are too low would mean that target groups would have to be widened considerably to achieve the required drawdown losses, and very low acceptance rates might result in extreme inefficiency of paying only renters. The move toward inefficiency is more gradual for higher than lower acceptance rates. Thus, hedging uncertainty might mean designing programs with at least 40–50 percent rates for lower YOS groups and 60–80 percent for higher YOS groups.

The plans analyzed here include the early retirement plan, three variants of the VSI plan, and two lump-sum separation plans. Our analysis of the acceptance rate by YOS for these plans reveals that four of the plans have acceptances far outside the ranges established above as efficient. Early retirement essentially has acceptance rates above 90 percent for all YOS, whereas nontransferable VSI with or without COLA and a lump sum of 2 x separation pay have unacceptably low acceptance rates—especially for higher YOS personnel. The two plans that come closest to achieving efficient acceptance rates are a lump sum of 2.5 x separation pay and transferable VSI without COLA.

The lump sum of 2.5 x separation pay comes closest to meeting the criteria of acceptance rates 70–80 for low YOS personnel and 40–60 for high YOS personnel. A lump sum slightly below 2.5—approximately 2.4—would place this program within the efficient criteria for all YOS groups. The transferable plan has acceptance rates for all YOS between 70–80 percent. A small reduction in the value of the transferable VSI would also provide efficient acceptance rates for most YOS groups. However, the lump-sum plan, because of its steeper slope as a function of YOS, probably allows lower payments for younger YOS personnel and would be preferable on grounds of efficiency.

A problem with all current plans is that they do not fit comfortably within the structure of current compensation and retirement programs. Currently, three programs pay individuals upon leaving military service: separation pay, voluntary separation payments (VSI, SSB), and military retirement. Separation pay is paid to individuals after 6 YOS who are involuntarily separated. Retirement is paid for those reaching 20 years of service. Individuals close to retirement will weigh separation incentives against their expected retirement annuity and benefits. However, more junior individuals when considering voluntary separation incentives may also include in their decision the possibility of involuntary separation and receiving separation pay.

Besides these expectations, questions of equity arise when designing a new program that will offer compensation to similar individuals who will receive either retirement or separation pay. Individuals who are involuntarily separated at 7 YOS will receive a lump sum of approximately $11,000. Voluntary separation offers may be made to individuals at the same YOS, and equity would dictate that these offers be at least as desirable as for those involuntarily separated, possibly with a comparable lump-sum payment. For individuals at 19 YOS, separation offers may need to look similar to the current retirement option. An offer with a large lump sum but no annuity at 19

YOS could create equity problems because individuals reaching 20 YOS would not have the option of a lump-sum substitute for retirement. Thus, those individuals who will be accepting voluntary separation offers will be similar to those receiving separation pay or retirement pay. This constrains the design of separation offers, if we want to provide nearly equivalent choices to similar individuals.

Hybrid plans that combine lump-sum payments and deferred annuities are able to meet these constraints. For lower YOS groups, the payments might be a lump sum equal to separation pay and a deferred annuity beginning at age 65. At 19 YOS the plan might offer a lump sum plus an annuity starting at an earlier age. This structure would make the lower YOS offer similar to separation pay but the higher YOS offer more like a retirement annuity. Our analysis has shown that the amount of the lump sum and the beginning of the annuity can be varied to achieve any desired acceptance rate. It could be shaped to provide lower acceptance rates for senior YOS and higher for junior YOS and still be in the "efficiency" range for each group.

A hybrid plan has several other advantages. It would avoid the long-term regret problem, since everyone would leave with a long-term annuity. A significant part of the value of such an offer would be in the lump-sum payment, and to this extent it would generate significant long-term savings for the government from the difference between the separation pay and retirement avoidance. Lump sums generate more of these savings because they take maximum advantage of the difference in discount rates. The annuity part of the payment would almost certainly be charged to the military retirement fund and not appear in DoD outlays. It would still be possible to offset the separation payments by accrual contribution reductions.

The hybrid plans contain elements of the plans favored by OSD, the Army, and the Air Force. This commonality might provide a basis of a compromise position supportable by all. The Air Force has favored lump sums, whereas the Army has favored early vesting. The original OSD VSI plan was an annuity that was cashable. This hybrid plan would provide some cash up front and an annuity. It could also contain provisions to include or exclude COLA as well as include or not include benefits. However, the main point is that once these kinds of decisions are made, the parameters of the plan can be set to achieve the desired acceptance-rate curves.

Finally, hybrid plans more easily address the problem of uncertainty in acceptance rates. The plan could, for instance, contain an annuity portion that could not be changed, but a lump-sum portion that could be empirically changed over time to achieve the desired acceptance rates. When the plan is announced, it would include a statement that the lump sum could increase or decrease over time depending on the initial acceptance rates. This is similar to bonus levels that are adjusted periodically up or down, and military personnel could accept this as an equitable feature, since it could go in either direction.

It is important to realize that any reasonable early separation offer (excluding the current early retirement offer) targeted to an appropriate group will bring net present value savings to the government. The savings depend primarily on two factors. The savings assume that:

- The difference in the discount rate between the government and those leaving is a real 4 percent, and

- The individuals leaving have at least an average chance of reaching retirement.

Those accepting separation offers will have the highest discount rates among their peers and would be willing to accept offers that are lower in present value than the current expected retirement. The average discount rate assumed here for individuals is a real rate of 12 percent. This rate substantially exceeds the assumed government rate of 4 percent. As long as the acceptance rates stay below 50 percent, we will be separating individuals with higher-than-average discount rates. Even above 50 percent acceptance, the difference in rates would be substantial. Lump-sum payments take maximum advantage of the difference between government and individual discount rates, whereas annuities provide long-term insurance.

The savings also depend on separating individuals with average or better retirement probabilities. Offers with very low acceptance rates risk losing money because many of the individuals leaving would be normal losses and would not have collected retirement annuities.

The choice of target groups can affect the retirement probabilities also. Targeting slower-promotion and lower-skill groups may bring higher-than-average retirement avoidance.

The disposition of these savings in the government budgeting process is an important decision because it will affect the incentives that the services have to separate these personnel. If the long-term savings are brought forward to cover the separation payment outlays and specifically given to the services making the separations, then the drawdown will not be adversely affected by the large outlays required for these payments. This adjustment can be accomplished through agreements between Congress and DoD about adjustments to the top DoD budget line. This line could reflect the net present value savings of such separations. Alternatively, the payments could be shifted to the military retirement fund that will receive the benefit of the retirement avoidance. Another solution would be to lower DoD retirement contributions and allow real offsets against separation payments. This approach would also need to involve adjustment of budget top lines, since the accrual payments are not part of the budget agreement.

The offer process must be monitored closely because adjustments in offer levels may be required if assumptions are not met. Careful monitoring of early results is needed to determine acceptance rates. These measurements are not straightforward, because only the observed acceptance rate is easy to determine. But the key parameter is the unobserved acceptance rate, which must include an empirically based estimate of normal attrition for each target group. Estimating this rate for each group will require surveys or research and models of retention from historical data.

The plan must contain a mechanism for adjustment that is equitable to individuals separating at different times. Adjustments can most easily be made in any lump-sum payment portion of the payment. The lump sum can be thought of as reverse bonus payments, and changing levels has precedent in the bonus program. Adjusting a lump sum rather than an annuity also provides more leverage, since decisions will be more sensitive to lump sums.

Finally, DoD and the services must provide sufficient support to assist people in making sound decisions. Soundly reasoned decisions are least likely to provoke second thought and long-term regret. This means providing the best promotion and pay information and financial counseling and allowing sufficient time for deliberation. A carrot-and-stick approach may be more likely to promote later regret. It could also raise questions of equitable treatment among service groups—by age, gender, or race. Every individual who voluntarily leaves early must be assured that the country appreciates his or her service and has terminated it taking due recognition of that contribution.

ESTIMATING PRESENT VALUES

We estimated present value using formulas in spreadsheets. Two present-value formulas were used depending on whether payments began at the beginning or end of the period. These formulas are:

$$P_v = \sum_{i=k}^{n} \frac{1}{(1-d)^i} p_i$$

where

    d = discount rate,
    p_i = payment in year i, and
    k = 0 if payment at beginning of period, and
    k = 1 if payment at end of period.

In comparing the present value of a separation payment to a retirement annuity, we initially assumed that the civilian income of those accepting separation payments exactly equaled their military pay had they stayed until retirement, and that postretirement pay was unaffected by whether the individual separated early or stayed until retirement. In this case, the comparison of present value is simply the present value of separation payments compared to the present value of military retirement (Figure 5.1, Figures 5.3–5.12). For SSB, the present value was simply equal to the lump-sum payment assumed to be paid upon separating. For VSI and other annuities, we assumed the income stream as specified in the plans. We assumed unless specified that the member would retire at 20 YOS as an E-6. We also assumed unless otherwise specified that the probability for reaching retirement was average for the YOS group (Figure 6.8). The reader can estimate the sensitivity of our results to alternative assumptions partly through Figure 5.12.

For military retirement, there are three distinct military retirement benefit categories for current active force members.

The initial benefit payment can be calculated for each of them by modifying the parameters in the formula

$$RET = m(YOS) \times (BPay) \qquad (1)$$

where

$$
\begin{aligned}
RET &= \text{initial annual retirement benefit,} \\
m(YOS) &= \text{initial multiplier,} \\
YOS &= \text{years of service, and} \\
Bpay &= \text{pay parameter.}
\end{aligned}
$$

The first category, FINAL PAY (FP), pertains to military members who entered the service *before September 8, 1980*. This provides the benefit calculated from Equation (1) with the retirement multiplier set equal to 2.5 percent x years of service and the pay parameter set equal to the final military basic pay received by the member. Years of service are capped at 30 in this formula so that a 20-year retiree receives 50 percent of his final basic pay as an initial benefit and a retiree with 30 or more years receives 75 percent of his final basic pay.

The second category, Hi-3, pertains to members who entered the service on or after September 8, 1980, and *before August 1, 1986*. The initial benefit value is obtained from Equation (1) by leaving the retirement multiplier unchanged, but changing the pay parameter to be equal to the average of the three years of highest base pay received by the member. Since basic pay increases monotonically throughout a career for most military members, we see that although both categories credit the retiree with 2.5 percent of his basic pay parameter per year of service, the Hi-3 method reduces the overall value of the initial retirement benefit by introducing a lower value for the basic pay parameter. Both categories cap years of service at 30 so that the retirement multiplier never exceeds 75 percent. The annual adjustment in benefits for both the FINAL PAY and Hi-3 categories equals the full COLA determined from the annual change in the CPI.

The third category, REDUX, applies to those entering the service *on or after August 1, 1986*, and further reduces the retirement benefit by penalizing temporarily those who retire before serving 30 years. It is obtained by reducing the retirement multiplier by 1 percent per full year of service under 30 at retirement. Thus a 20-year retiree would have a multiplier of 40 percent instead of the 50 percent given by the other methods, whereas a 30-year retiree would still have a 75 percent multiplier. The penalty is temporary because the multiplier is restored to the same value used in the other methods when the retiree reaches age 62.

REDUX also calculates Bpay by averaging the three years of highest base pay. Not only is the initial benefit lower, but retirement benefits grow more slowly for retirees in the REDUX group. Their annual benefit adjustment is obtained by subtracting 1 percent from the full COLA used by the other categories. Although a one-time catch-up payment is applied when they reach age 62, the reduced annual adjustments continue thereafter. Overall, REDUX retirees can expect a significantly lower stream of total retirement benefits than retirees in the other categories.

Comparisons were also made assuming different civilian pay assumptions (Figure 5.12). We assumed that the civilian pay of those leaving intially dropped 15 percent below their military pay had they stayed. This difference was linearly reduced to zero over 5 years. It was then assumed that the civilian pay of those leaving early was 5 percent above their military pay and/or civilian pay after retirement for the remainder of their working life.

In the latter calculations, we assumed that the member's military pay would be the average for the YOS group, and retirement would be as an E-6 unless otherwise specified.

Asch, Beth J., and Warner, John T., *A Policy Analysis of Alternative Military Retirement Systems*, RAND, MR-465-OSD, 1994.

Beland, Russell, "The Senior Career Force and the Drawdown," a draft report prepared for the Assistant Secretary of Defense (Force Management and Personnel), March 13, 1991.

Beland, Russell, "Voluntary Separations by the Senior Career Force as a Tool in the Drawdown," a briefing prepared for the Assistant Secretary of Defense (Force Management and Personnel), April 15, 1991.

Black, Matthew, *Personal Discount Rates: Estimates for the Military Population*, study prepared for the Fifth Quadrennial Review of Military Compensation, Systems Research and Applications Corporation, May 1983.

Cylke, Stephen, Matthew S. Goldberg, Paul Hogan, and Lee Mairs, *Estimation of the Personal Discount Rate: Evidence from Military Reenlistment Decisions*, Center for Naval Analyses, Professional Paper 356, April 1982.

Daula, Thomas, and Robert Moffitt, "Estimating Dynamic Models of Quit Behavior: The Case of Military Retirement," 1992.

Doering, Zahava D., and William P. Hutzler, *Description of Officers and Enlisted Personnel in the U.S. Armed Forces: A Reference for Military Manpower Analysis*, RAND, R-2851-MRAL, March 1982.

Grissmer, David, and Bernard Rostker, "Military Manpower in a Changing World," in Joseph Kruzel (ed.), *American Defense Annual*, Lexington Books, New York, 1992.

Landsberger, Michael, "Consumer Discount Rate and the Horizon: New Evidence," *Journal of Political Economy*, Vol. 79, pp. 1346–1359, 1971.

McCain, John, member of the Senate Armed Services Committee, letter to the Assistant Secretary of Defense (Force Management and Personnel), June 21, 1991.

"Military Voluntary Separation Incentive Act," Draft Bill and Section-by-Section Analysis prepared for the Speaker of the House of Representatives by the Office of the Assistant Secretary of Defense (Force Management and Personnel), July 1991.

Report of the President's Commission on Military Compensation, submitted to President Carter, April 1978.

Senate Armed Services Committee (SASC), report on the *National Defense Authorization Act for Fiscal Year 1992, Title IV—Military Personnel Authorizations, Part A—Active Forces*, July 1991.